Gaile,

Here's another one republished
this year — it may not be
your cup of tea but I'd like
it to be on your shelf

Love
Jim

Strategy in
Poker, Business
and War

John McDonald
Cranberry, September 12, 1985

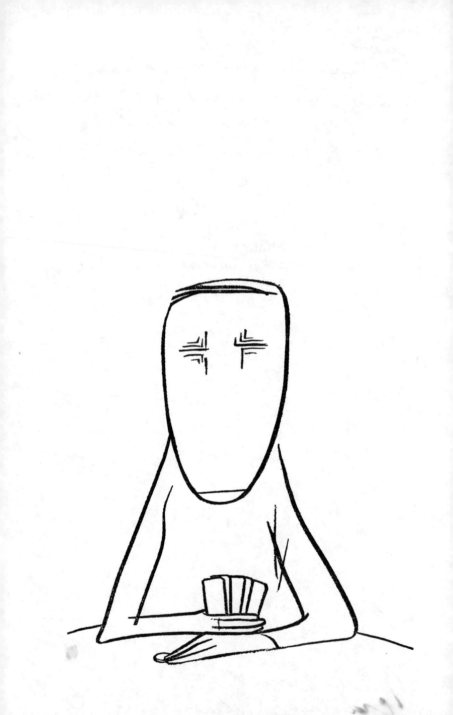

Strategy in Poker, Business and War

By JOHN McDONALD

Illustrated by ROBERT OSBORN

W · W · NORTON & COMPANY

New York · London

Books That Live
The Norton imprint on a book means that in the publisher's
estimation it is a book not for a single season but for the years.
W. W. Norton & Company, Inc.

ISBN 0-393-00225-X

W. W. Norton & Company, Inc., 500 Fifth Avenue, New York, N. Y. 10110
W. W. Norton & Company Ltd., 37 Great Russell Street, London WC1B 3NU

PRINTED IN THE UNITED STATES OF AMERICA

3 4 5 6 7 8 9 0

Contents

TO

"OUR WIVES, POOR WRETCHES"

verbally and discussed with me the mathematical text of the theory. Later he made valued criticisms of this study. Oswald Jacoby, the bridge champion and authority on card games, contributed a number of suggestions on the actual game of poker. From that time until after I published a second article on the subject in *Fortune*, called "A Theory of Strategy" (June, 1949), I received valuable assistance from many other distinguished individuals. My former colleague at *Fortune*, Professor J. K. Galbraith of Harvard University, followed the study continuously with advice on economic and editorial questions. Professor John W. Tukey, mathematician of Princeton University, read drafts of the articles and the book, and made comments and suggestions. Dr. E. W. Paxson of the Rand Corporation, Professor E. J. Gumbel of the New School for Social Research, Professor Herbert A. Simon of the Illinois Institute of Technology, W. Edward Deming of the U.S. Bureau of the Budget, and Professor Jacob Marschak of the Cowles Commission, University of Chicago, read one or another manuscript of the articles in work, and generously made criticisms and suggestions, many of which have found their way into the book. Dr. Gunnar Boe, former Norwegian representative of the U.N. Economic and Employment Commission, gave time to discussion of game theory. Ruth Miller of the *Fortune* staff contributed intensive research assistance on the subject of monopoly; Mia Fritsch assisted in studying the background of poker. Mary Grace, chief proofreader at *Fortune*, kindly put her fine-tooth comb through the text. And there are many others who have discussed with me one or another part of this work, whom I must thank in person.

The two articles on which this book is based were the property of *Fortune* magazine. I am grateful to the editors, and in particular to the publisher, C. D. Jackson, for turning them over to me along with the research, for book publication. I am especially indebted to the managing editor, Ralph D. Paine, who was the patron and editor of those articles.

I am, of course, alone responsible for this result.

Robert Osborn makes his own counterpoint with his well-known pen.

—JMcD

INTRODUCTION

In the literature of social conflict, an exact description of the nature of strategy has been wanting, Machiavelli and Clausewitz notwithstanding. No English dictionary defines the term except in the narrow military sense. Machiavelli saw truly that strategy is pervasive in human affairs. In *The Prince* he tells how deception is an essential element in the making of a fortune or the winning of a political or military campaign. Unfortunately for his reputation he did not separate his objective appraisal from the ethical difficulties that clung to it (he was specifically interested in the unification of Italy), and he became immortalized as the political cynic, despite the efforts of a number of philosophers to show the integrity of his vision.

Clausewitz, the master of modern military science, looked upon war as a continuation of politics on another level. His essay, *Principles of War,* finds the essence of the military situation in uncertainty: "Not only are we uncertain about the strength of the enemy, but in addition rumor (i.e., all the news which we obtain from outposts, through spies, or by accident) exaggerates his size. The majority of people are timid by nature, and that is why they constantly exaggerate danger. All influences on the military leader, therefore, combine to give him a false impression of his opponent's strength, and from this arises a new source of indecision . . . We cannot take this uncertainty too seriously, and it is important to be prepared for it from the beginning." To be prepared is to have a policy, that is, a strategy. And "We must never lack calmness and firmness . . . We must therefore familiarize

ourselves with the thought of an honorable defeat." Honorable defeats disappeared in the last war, but the notion that winning is a function of the idea of losing is a psychological subtlety which may be compared with a more concrete "pessimistic" assumption to be found later in this book. Clausewitz, however, does not provide a general theory of strategy. He stays within the confines of military situations, which, as will be seen, are generally narrower and less complex than economic and political situations.

The concept of strategy presented here is new in the history of human thought. It was originated by one of the chief participants in the development of the atomic bomb, the young and already great contemporary mathematician, John von Neumann, and developed in collaboration with the eminent economist, Oskar Morgenstern, under the title, *Theory of Games and Economic Behavior*. It is not and never can be available in its entirety to the layman, for it is written largely in the special notation of the mathematician. There is nothing mathematical, however, in the observations to be found here. It is sufficient in this connection simply to note that the key conceptions were discovered by that rigorous medium of logic. Only the familiar language of ideas in words will be found in this book.

Imperfect information creates uncertainty among individuals in games and in society. One has only to reflect on the relations between partners at the bridge table or opponents in poker; or on the traders in stock and commodity markets, or the housewife on a shopping tour, to see the characteristic of uncertainty. Where uncertainty exists strategies are employed to clarify or further obscure the information. The theory of games therefore deals with deception, particularly counterdeception, as a common strategy, and with strategies of clarification. Yet the theory is formal and neutral, non-ideological, as good for one man as for another. Although deeply involved in the mysteries of value, it does not intrude on the province of ethics; nor can it tell anyone his desires. But it may be able to tell what one can get and how one can get it.

Like all economic theories, the theory of games is based on the assumption that man seeks gain (alternative assumptions belong to psychology, sociology, anthropology and other sciences). The theory of games also assumes, however, that man is rational, whereas it is generally believed that man is more often irrational. The "player" here must be willing to forgo maximum desires, to remember that he is not, like Robinson Crusoe, alone in what he wants. In seeking gain, he must be willing and able to

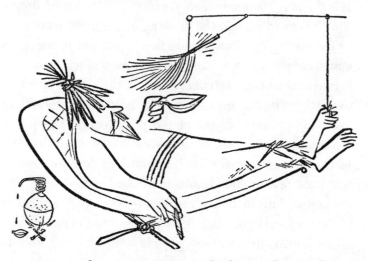

recognize and come to terms with the conflicting desires and actions of others. If the theory of games can be said to focus on one thing, it is the common fallacy that the rational individual is able to reach an unlimited maximum goal in society.

Common sense is often frustrated in an attempt to maximize two interdependent desires. The concept of "the greatest possible good for the greatest possible number" represented the best social sentiment of a majority of people for a long time (it is still a useful weapon of political deception). Yet, as will be seen, only Robinson Crusoe can achieve the greatest possible good for the greatest possible number, the number being one. In place of the notion represented by this aphorism, the theory of games establishes the concept of a strategy through which conflicting maximum desires can be reconciled in an optimum. It is the only economic theory, except that based on Robinson Crusoe, to explain the working of the profit motive.

The strategical situation in game theory lies in the interaction between two or more persons, each of whose actions is based on an expectation concerning the actions of others over whom he has no control. The outcome is dependent upon the personal moves of the participants. The policy followed in making these moves is strategy. Both the military strategist and the businessman act continuously in this state of suspended animation. And regardless of the amount of information given them—short of the ideal of perfect information—they generally act in the final analysis on hunch; that is, they gamble without being able to calculate the risk.

For example, a duel. Two men back to back, each with a pistol and one bullet. They walk away from each other a certain number of paces, turn and . . . fire or begin walking back toward each other. At the farthest distance apart the chances of a hit are less than with each pace back toward the opponent. To fire and miss would be to give the opponent a sure kill at any range he chooses. To hold fire would be to risk being shot before having an opportunity to shoot. Thus two maximums conflict: to have the first shot or to have a better shot. The dueler cannot have both. The question then is when to shoot with optimum strategical value.

Given the distances and marksmanships of the duelers, this problem has been solved in precise terms by the theory of games. The traditional duel is a model for a number of military situations, not the least of which is that of two airplanes entering each other's range in combat. It is also the problem of dueling tanks, where the situation may be complicated by "silent guns," which hide the actual shooting until a hit is made. "Silent guns" covers all cases in which a combatant does not know when his opponent has fired, whether the guns are actually noiseless or not. The theory is familiarly known to the military as "Games," though its high security classification wherever it has actual content is a sign that its intent is anything but trifling. A young scientist attached to the Air Forces said recently of its military application, "We hope it will work, just as we hoped in 1942 that the atomic bomb would work."

In business likewise there are conflicting maximums. Buyer and seller, for example, must reconcile their desires in a price. As the late great British economist, John Maynard Keynes, once observed, "Businessmen play a mixed game of skill and chance, the average results of which to the players are not known by those who take a hand." The same can be said of the political and economic moves of industry, labor, and farm organization leaders; or the moves of leaders in domestic and international politics. The theory of games is designed to narrow this gamble to the point where it would be irrational to act other than by a known, optimum policy (strategy). It tries to make the imponderable ponderable.

Before too much is expected, however, it should be said that the theory of games is spectacular, if that is the word, only in an intellectual sense, and only in that sense can it be appreciated.

Although based on the mathematical theory of games, this book is rather an interpretation of the theory than a rendering of it. The general essay on poker at the beginning is intended to lay the foundation and atmosphere for what follows; perhaps enough explanation of the game is given in passing to get the uninitiated through without too much difficulty.

PART ONE

Poker, the Game

CONSIDER how a number of free men gather around in a somewhat friendly atmosphere of blue smoke and blue chips, and, rapt in study of five dealt cards, proceed throughout the night to engage in a contest of strategies, governed by unique rules, for the purpose of securing a part of one another's substance. This is poker, stud or draw, or, as some say, open or closed: one card down and four up or all in hand with a drawing to improve the composition. Each man is privy alone to the secret of his own hand; he knows the rest only as money talks. No one could be more surprised or shocked than the players themselves to discover that in this ritual of poker night may lie a clue to problems that have puzzled economists for a long time. Yet what scientists since Aristotle have tried and failed to do has all the time been done by the gamecocks of mankind, and that is to design a "controlled experiment" of human action, a kind of laboratory of man's experience. Like the law of gravity and all great thoughts, it is quite simple and has always been in plain view. The laboratory is the *game*, and the laboratory of capitalism, and of socialism too for that matter, is poker.

The real substance of poker is not cards but money. Its spirit is the bluff; its supreme objective the inducement of a bet against an "immortal" (unbeatable) hand. Poker thus is a game of strategies in which the cards of agreed-upon rank and sanction are the instrument. Their random distribution according to the luck of the deal, known only fragmentarily by their respective holders, creates the chancy situation from which to proceed. Money exerts the discipline of real value. The strategy of the bluff raises poker to a high plane of conflict. And winning a bet achieves the aim of the game, the acknowledged triumph over an opponent. How unrepentant one is at this conclusion!

The play of the cards can be learned from books, but it is usually learned by experience from old hands at the price of lost pots. The game is more difficult to describe, in its deeper aspects, than it is to play—as evidenced by the fact that it is picked up naturally and with considerable subtlety by all classes and ages of men. It has been handed down with variations from poker players to poker players since it was created in New Orleans more than a hundred years ago. It was played in the United States during its first fifty years without any codification, players merely synchronizing their habits, as they still do, before beginning the game. Although many books on poker have been written to correct this situation, there is still no universally accepted Hoyle of poker, as there is of bridge. And yet the basic game is universally known.

Poker is the most skillful of all card games in the view of Oswald Jacoby, champion bridge player and the leading contemporary authority on poker. He distinguishes poker on the principle that it concerns the management of money, whereas other card games concern the management of cards. "In bridge," he observes, "if your opponents hold certain cards they can bid and make a grand slam and all you can do is pay. Likewise in gin if your opponent goes gin before you get a play you are equally helpless. In poker if an opponent holds a royal flush, he is going to win the pot, if any; but, if you are smart enough to figure out that he holds it, you do not have to call his bet."

A knowledge of mathematical probabilities will not make a good poker player, but a total disregard for them will make a bad one. Every poker player knows better than to draw to an inside straight; yet few can resist drawing to an open-end straight, which is also generally inadvisable, since the probability of making it is but eight in

forty-seven, and if you do make it, one of your opponents may do better. The anonymous gamesters who created the game, however, were gifted with a mathematical intuition by which they set the rank of the hands—after some confusion about flushes—in proper accord with the laws of probability. All poker, excepting wild games, is played within the finite framework of 2,598,960 hands, arranged in rank corresponding to the following theoretical frequency and probability of appearance (without benefit of a draw).

Straight flush	40	(or once in	64,974 hands)
Four of a kind	624	(or once in	4,165 hands)
Full house	3,744	(or once in	694 hands)
Flush	5,108	(or once in	509 hands)
Straight	10,200	(or once in	256 hands)
Three of a kind	54,912	(or once in	48 hands)
Two pair	123,552	(or once in	21 hands)
One pair	1,098,240	(or once in	2½ hands)
Other hands	1,302,540	(or once in	2 hands)
Total	2,598,960		

All poker calculations must begin with this fundamental scheme.

Many probability calculations are used in poker—but it is a rare player who tries to calculate very closely. Getting the range is usually sufficient to the occasion, as the play is fast and *card* probability is only one of several calculations involved. There is, for example, the ratio of the amount already in the pot to the amount you must pay in bets to stay in. And beyond that there are the multiple strategies involved in the play of opponents.

The key to good poker is the setting of the stake. Ersatz poker can be played with valueless chips if the players are exceptionally gifted in fantasy. But any false stake is ruinous to the game—a matter more of attitude than of the absolute amount: for good play depends on respect for the chips. A low limit reduces the value of bluffing and thereby saps the vitality of any strategy. Unduly low limits lead to straight gambling on chance cards, as in faro or blackjack. Unduly high limits result in erratic play— extremes of timidity and bravado—and such financial damage to the players as to disqualify the play as a game. A sound limit is the lowest possible sum that all the players will respect, from a newsboy's penny to a rich man's blank check—a most difficult common denominator to achieve, as all poker players know. This is the question of morale, without which poker is a bore. The best high-limit game is table stakes, in which one may "tap" another player for as much as the full amount in sight before him on the table. But going from a regular limit to table stakes is like going from elementary geography to astronomy, and likewise requires advanced study. Unlimited poker is not a game but a duel executed with money instead of pistols.

All varieties of poker take either of two basic forms, draw or stud. That is, either you are given the opportunity to improve your original hand by discarding and drawing new cards, or you must play the original hand. The five essential movements of draw poker, anteing, dealing, betting before the draw (or dropping out), discarding and drawing, and betting again after the draw, give the game a special complexity. Since the draw puts more cards into play, the hands often run the whole gamut of rank and make for spectacular play.

The variation of jackpots appeared in the late nineteenth century, and, according to one story, developed out of a protracted game of draw played by a group in Toledo in 1870. The players had become so conservative as never to open with less than jacks. They then made it a rule that only jacks or better could open the play, and added the stinger that an ante must first be made by all players. Thus if the jackpot opener failed to get a bet, he had the consolation of reaping the considerable pot formed by the antes. Jackpots is a more chanceful game than straight draw. With a streak of cards too low to put into play, one can lose substantially in antes. And when—as often happens—several deals go by without an opener, the pot grows to such proportions as to make it advisable when it is opened to come in on a long shot with almost any cards. Tight players eschew the game. But in the old days it used often to be played episodically as a concession to liberal players, with a penknife placed in a regular pot, the winner of which dealt jackpots when his turn came around. The knife, with a typical buckhorn handle, has been much used to designate the dealer in poker. A declination could be made by "passing the buck," the origin of the expression. In *The Gentleman's Handbook of Poker*, a standard work written over the pseudonym "Florence" in 1892 and now

26

a collector's item, the comment is added that a knife is not an obligatory buck. "In the Far West a revolver on the table sometimes serves the purpose . . ."

Stud poker is fast, tight, and almost purely strategical. With one card turned down and four showing, the unknown element in each player's hand is at a minimum and each round of open cards produces a series of simple, clear correlation probabilities, and leaves the real play to the representations made by the players. This fine-drawn game, originated, according to one old source, by the Negroes of New Orleans not long before they produced that other great American invention, jazz music, is played in low key as far as the hands go. Seldom rising above two pair or three of a kind, they are generally played with high card or single pair; and when there are several players, some of them are often frozen out before they obtain a complete hand of five cards. Stud is the game for those who like their poker neat.

Many variations of poker have been forgotten and new ones constantly appear. Wild cards, additional hand combinations without end, such as dog, tiger, skeet, blaze, and low ball, and different modes of play combine to make variations—each popular, usually, in a certain region of the country. Most of them tend to jazz up the game, increasing the chance element and decreasing the strategy. A game whose value is much disputed is seven-card stud, high-low. The deal—two down, four up, and one down, as in regular seven-card stud, but with both high and low hand winning and dividing the pot—makes an excellent game for liveliness, attracting much play. Purists among poker players generally look down on it for that reason. One of the most celebrated of poker games, played by "The Thanatopsis Literary and Inside Straight Club" during the 1920's, foundered for lack of a chart through the hazards of this game. Among the players were Alexander Woollcott, Harpo Marx, Russel Crouse, Herbert Swope, Heywood Broun, and Franklin P. Adams. "The Thanatopsis struck a reef and sank with few survivors . . ." says F.P.A. "The reef was seven-card stud, and high-low stud at that. In that ruinous game, it takes great patience to wait until you have a good hand, especially as a bad hand may be the best." Thanatopsis must be considered a sacrifice to pioneering. Jacoby now recommends the game as sound *if you always play for low* and take high only as a consolation should it come by chance.

The bluff, as suggested earlier, is the spirit of poker. Its fundamental object is to create uncertainty between the players. In poker one has cards, chips, and conversation. The cards are known only to their holder, who "represents" their value to his opponents in the form of chips bet and comments made. When the representation is false, that is bluffing. If there were no such misrepresentation, the highest bet would always signify the highest hand and the lower hands would always decline the issue. There would then never be any real betting and hence no game, unless it were arranged to make a pool for the player with the highest hand. Many poker games for one reason or another degenerate to this level, where they are no longer poker but ordinary gambling. In the real game one never knows what cards opponents may be holding except by analysis of strategies.

The principal form of bluffing is to represent a low hand as high, especially when the circumstances favor such misrepresentation. The object here superficially is to win the pot by forcing the retirement of a higher hand; but should this fail, as may often be expected, and one is caught in the bluff, its higher purpose is realized in the confusion that such a play causes in the minds of one's opponents with regard to future representations. The game thus is dynamic and depends upon a series of plays, as a result of which, when one's hand is strong, it will be suspected of weakness and a large bet will be forthcoming.

Bluffing, however, is hazardous and expensive and must be so calculated as either to win or to cost relatively little. The player who never bluffs seldom gets a big bet and many of his best hands go abegging. He is inevitably a loser. The player who bluffs often and expensively is unable to retrieve the loss. He also is a loser. Since all the players are engaging in the practice of bluffing, confusion is rampant at the poker table and close attention must be paid to the pace of the game, the laws of probability, the habits of each player, and the situations that develop to give one or another of the players the advantage.

The corollary of bluffing is calling the bluff. Here again variation is the play. A man who always calls is rarely bluffed, and that might be a distinction if it were not that as a result all his calls will be against strong hands, and he will

always lose. Likewise a man who always drops in the face of strong representation will always lose, for he will be bluffed off the table.

Thus the mark of good poker playing is deception. The poker hand must at all times be concealed behind the mask of inconsistency. The good poker player must avoid set practices and act at random, going so far, on occasion, as to violate the elementary principles of correct play. The pace of the player must be suited to the company, tight in a tight game, liberal in a liberal game—though a player may be strong enough to bull the whole play. When a good player thinks he has a winning hand, he makes the kill with more powerful action than a conservative player would believe

prudent. And Baron Rothschild's maxim is useful: "Cut short your losses; let your profits run on."

One of the greatest bluffs in history—a poker legend that persisted throughout the second half of the nineteenth century—took place in a game between Henry Clay and Daniel Webster. Webster was dealing draw. Clay drew one card and Webster stood pat. The stake was unlimited and the game became interesting as Webster bet high and Clay raised. After several reraises there was $4,000 in the pot and Clay called. As it is told in *The Gentleman's Handbook of Poker*, Webster laughed, shrugged his shoulders, and threw his hand on the pot, saying, "I've only a pair of deuces."

"Then the pot is yours," said Clay, also laughing. "I have only ace high."

Clay's call was so inexcusable that poker critics have doubted the story. Clay had a high reputation as a poker player, and it seems unlikely that he would have risen above a ward heeler with such reasoning. For after Webster bet, Clay's raise might have been sound enough since it could have driven Webster out. By all odds it should have; he was holding a hand only a shade better than ace high. Each clearly and correctly suspected the other of bluffing. Still *in no case should either player have called,* for neither could reasonably have desired to match his low hand against even a bluffed hand. No amount of knowledge of each other's bluffing tactics could justify anything but infinite raising or retirement without seeing. The story long had currency not only because of the participants but because it portrays the ultimate in bluff and a classic boner in play.

Jacoby tells a story that is quite different. The players included Alan Blount, reputedly one of the best poker players in the U.S. around the turn of the century, and Jacoby's father. This one is difficult. The game was draw, $20 limit, $5 ante.

"The first player opened, Blount stayed as did another player and father raised. The opener stayed for the raise, Blount reraised, the other player dropped, father raised again and the opener and Blount stayed so that there was exactly $300 in the pot before the draw. The opener drew one, Blount and father drew two and it was checked to father who bet. The opener dropped, Blount raised, father raised, Blount raised a second time, father did likewise, Blount studied awhile and said, 'I drop, your four aces are good,' and showed that he held four kings. Father had the four aces all right.

"Here is Blount's reasoning. 'Jacoby is a good conservative player. When I raised him back before the draw he knew that I held at least a fairly large set of three of a kind. With two large pair or a small three of a kind he knew I would have raised immediately. Hence when he raised a second time and then drew two cards he clearly showed either three kings, three aces or a desperate bluff. His subsequent action showed that he wasn't bluffing. I held kings myself so he must have started with three aces. My raise after the draw clearly showed that I had made at least a full house, his reraise showed that he had filled also, my second raise clearly indicated that I had made four of a kind so that his second raise indicated four of a kind also. Since I know he has aces, and know he has four of them, my four kings are no good and there is no point in my wasting an additional $20 on them.' "

This story is told to show that one should never throw good money after bad. And it also illustrates the similar principle that one should never "respect a good hand." All hands except the "immortal" are relative and, no matter how high, may stand beaten at some point in the play. The story is as extreme as the Clay-Webster one, for Blount is the only man ever reported to have had such confidence in his analysis as to refrain from a $20 call in face of a pot of more than $300 and a hand with four kings. Only Blount's reputation as a poker player will make the story reasonable to the ordinary mortal. He had more to gain than the pot. But of Henry Clay it can only be said that his Jacksonian enemies must have planted the story for just such an occasion as this.

Poker and American history are inseparable. Like everything American, poker's antecedents were mixed. Some elements of poker are believed to come from As Nas, an ancient Persian card game, others from Poque, a French game. Its English cousin is Brag, and another French cousin is Ambigu. The whole family of bragging games in the West derived from an Italian game, Primiera, from which it disappears into antiquity, probably along the gypsy trail by which playing cards were brought into Europe from the East in the fifteenth century. The theory of poker's earliest history lies in a single study ably written for the New York *Sun* on May 22, 1904, the author of which is presumed to be

34

the late Robert E. Foster, chief "Mr. Hoyle" of the U.S. for the past fifty years. The conjuncture of As Nas and Poque is thought to have taken place among sailors in New Orleans in the early nineteenth century and the Americans are believed to have made their customary mispronunciation of French by dividing Poque into two syllables, thus: Po-que, later corrupted to poker. Poque was played with hands of three cards from a deck of thirty-two and contained such combinations as pairs and three of a kind. The Persians played their As Nas "poker" with hands of five cards from a twenty-card deck whose cards ranked: lion, king, lady, soldier, and dancing girl. Hence the theory, never proved, that As Nas was grafted onto Poque, with the Western deck of aces and court cards, to form the original twenty-card New Orleans poker. The play at first was showdown and some of the present combinations were missing. The draw and the full deck were soon added; jackpots, stud, and straights and flushes came much later.

From New Orleans, poker went up the Mississippi River with the steamboats, and by the 1840's was the principal card game of the frontier. The gambling spirit was so much a part of the frontiersman's character that the game overlapped into life. Poker was often played for unlimited stakes. Plantations, slaves, gold mines, and fortunes, according to legend, backed up a man's opinion at the table. If a bet was higher than a man's resources, he had, by a universally accepted rule, twenty-four hours to raise call money—during which the cards were sealed and held by an arbiter. Poker and professional gamblers became as much a part of American folklore as cowboys and Indians, sheriffs and bad men. It did not achieve even moderate respectability until after the Civil War.

Then in the gambling boom that accompanied the era of fortune seeking, poker came into its golden age. The Honorable Robert Schenck, a political and poker-playing colleague of both Clay and Webster, during his ambassadorship to Great Britain (1872) gave the game a certain cachet when, as the story goes, he showed Queen Victoria how to play at a royal party in Somersetshire. The Queen asked him to write down the rules. Ambassador Schenck obliged and sometime later one of the gentlemen present ran it off on his private printing press. A copy of this leaked to the American press. Poker at court! They called him "Poker Schenck" and he was much embarrassed in the ensuing scandal. Schenck had had a rough trip in politics, including a mining scandal in which he appears to have been equally innocent. But he had been scheduled to be laid quietly away in the scholars'

books before this poker favor ensured his immortality. For his was the first codification of poker in history, the founding classic of the game.*

Thereafter this game for exchanging real fortunes became a game of fortune to be won by luck, science, and intuitive skill, in a combination unexampled except in life itself. It spread throughout the world and came into its present estate as the favorite card game among men in the U.S. The public expressed its kinship with the game by absorbing its language. Every American, poker player or not, knows what it is to have an ace in the hole (or up the sleeve) or to be in the chips, to bluff or call a bluff, stand pat, four-flush, put his cards on the table, have a showdown, or otherwise get into a situation where the chips are down; and finally to meet the end of life itself by cashing in his chips.

Man is so eternally busy being about his father's business that he has generally found it necessary to defend both art and play—on more or less the same grounds—for being out of the context of "life." There is some justification for the distinction since real life generally ends in an action that has

* The only known copy of the royal original was destroyed in the British Museum during the past war. The rare-book room of the New York Public Library has a copy of the first regular "edition" published in New York in 1875: an eight-page flimsy, the size of a playing card. Among some of the U.S. poker classics that followed Schenck's were John Blackbridge's *The Complete Poker Player* (1875), Henry T. Winterblossom's *The Game of Draw Poker* (1875), Richard A. Proctor's *Poker Principles and Chance Laws* (1883), and John W. Keller's *The Game of Draw Poker* (1887). The wittiest book on poker, written in the style of W. C. Fields, is Garrett Brown's *How to Beat the Game* (1903), out of print and extremely rare.

immediate consequences, whereas art and play appear more to be ends in themselves with no apparent actionable crisis in the outcome. Most of the ways of tying art to life resolve themselves into two, one originating in Plato, who thought art should serve a social purpose, the other originating in Aristotle, who thought that it might have some purgative effect on the evil in man. Plato thought that on seeing tragedy in the theatre, a man might be inspired to go out and kill somebody. Aristotle thought that having performed the assassination in his heart, the man—through pity and fear—was purged of excessive emotion that had failed to be discharged in the actions of life. Traditionally this difference has arrayed the Puritans and "proletarians" against the Cavaliers and liberals—an odd crosshatch on the surface of history.

There is no literature of play comparable in richness to the literature of art, but it is obvious that games, especially competitive games, are subject in some degree to the same divergence of opinion. Those of a Platonist turn of mind

will regard poker as good or bad on the emulative principle; the Aristotelians on the purgative principle. The poker player's joy at bluffing his opponent, accordingly, is either a poor exercise in social conduct or a valuable spill-over of latent desire. And the excitement of winning a big pot either teaches avarice or expends it like smoke in the air.

But poker must be distinguished from other gambling games. All gambling tends toward either a test of luck or a test of skill. In roulette or dice, for example, skill is wholly eliminated. Man, devoid of all secular capacity except cajolery, and all knowledge of cause and effect except the laws of probability, places himself before the unknown and seeks grace of the deity Fortune. He talks to the dice or makes a

system at roulette, imploring favor. He wears charms, tips beggars, won't eat peanuts before a race if he is a jockey, alternates incantations with silent blasphemy, all to seek the mystic rhythm of the universe and determine its future—a

chosen man whose distinction will be symbolized by the substance of his win. On losing he is not only dejected; worse, his appeals ignored, he feels rejected. No one who is not a gambler knows the depths to which he is thrown by Fortune's refusal to give her love. But on the way home he recovers. What a man to have braved Fortune, to have the fortitude to stand alone against Fortune's persecution! And then he can try it over, find the key, open the door, tempt her again. And if he wins? Everyone remembers Dostoevski's obsessed gambler who granted that if he should make the world's greatest fortune at the wheel he would spend it

all quickly in Paris and return again to the table for the ecstasy of another win. He but dramatized man's centuries-old persistence in resisting the efforts of reformers to destroy the instinct.

The relationship between the gambler and the primitive has been noted in anthropology, with the suggestion that the gambling instinct derives from man's precultural history. The primitive lives but does not contest his fate. If war is contemplated, he will consult the divining rod or some other sign. If the gods should signify favor, war becomes merely an administrative action. But if a lot of his

people get killed he quits and runs, not from cowardice, but because he has read the signs wrongly. The gods really favored the other side. This was not "luck," but fate—a decision against him from which there was no appeal.

Of all the gambling games known to man, poker is the least given to such primitive idolatry. Sin, perhaps, in departing from Christ's example of giving rather than taking, but not heresy. In poker, man contests with man; in the long run, luck should even itself out. The game is a travesty on life, and as such it reveals some of the moral and psychological secrets of men (women at poker reveal mainly their curiosity, and curiosity in poker is fatal). Shrewdness, cunning, deception, conscious strategies, suspicious appraisals of worth and character, and bold aggressions, all the repressed values of a competitive society are let loose and placed first in the order of proprieties. Hope, yes, and an honesty redefined to make room for certain types of deception. But brotherhood? Faith? Charity? These are the least of the qualities of a good poker player.

That poker has seemed on occasion less like a game than an extension of the corrupt practices of life itself is perhaps one reason why it is customary for poker players to settle accounts at the conclusion of play. If there is any difficulty, the error is not in the nature of the game but in playing too hard, an inadmissible garbling of the graces of life (someone is bound to lose his shirt once in a while). The game that ends in an action that extends to life itself may be a game, but it is not play.

Beyond what he can pay for his pleasure, the reasonable man will give some credence to the classical economic theory of gambling. This theory—applicable to games, markets, or business, and the theoretical basis of progressive taxation—originates in the observation of the great

45

eighteenth-century mathematician, Daniel Bernoulli, to the effect that the value of an amount of money to a man varies according to the amount he already has. Alfred Marshall (*Principles of Economics*), perhaps the leading economist of a generation ago, developed this doctrine of "declining marginal utility" to say that, with the odds even and the game square, a given sum of money has not the same value when won as it has when lost. The winner, that is, cannot win as much as the loser loses and gambling thus involves an economic loss.

This led to some amusing speculation by John Maynard Keynes in *A Treatise on Probability:* "The gambler is in a worse position if his capital is smaller than his opponents'— at poker, for instance, or on the Stock Exchange. This is clear. But our desire for moral improvement outstrips our logic if we tell him that he *must* lose. Besides it is paradoxical to say that everybody individually must lose and that everybody collectively must win. For every individual gambler who loses there is an individual gambler or syndicate of gamblers who wins. The true moral is this, that poor men should not gamble and that millionaires should do nothing else. But millionaires gain nothing by gambling with one another, and until the poor man departs from the path of prudence the millionaire does not find his opportunity."

If the loss is more than the gain, why then do gamblers go on gambling? * The answer is one that cannot be written

* The social realities are being more closely examined in scientific thought today. A notable study on risk-taking made by Milton Friedman

in Bernoulli's language. There is something else at work here. Anatole France (*The Garden of Epicurus*) explained it in his comment on two shipwrecked sailors shooting craps on the back of a whale: "And in very deed there is something in play that does terribly stir the fibers of daring hearts. Is it an insignificant delight to tempt fortune? Is it a pleasure devoid of intoxication to taste in one second, months, years, a whole lifetime of fears and hopes?"

The impulse to gamble remains as an aspect of the apparently ineradicable irrationality of modern man. On this idea of his nature is based the theory of incentive in the economics of capitalism, that he produces more and survives best under the risks of competition. It matters not for the moment that business competition is productive as well as speculative, whereas gambling, as Dr. Johnson defined it, is "the mode of transferring property without any intermediate good." For the gambling impulse is the same whether exercised in play or as an element in real life.

But man celebrates himself more for the other side of his nature. By taking thought he has sought to impose restrictions on his gambling instincts. He has tried with consider-

---

and L. J. Savage (*Journal of Political Economy*, August, 1948) shows that the same people buy insurance and lottery tickets, even though lotteries are unfair games of chance. It is observed too that people crowd into glittering, fame-and-fortune businesses and professions where the total number of members divided into the total earnings is less than the wage of a modest but secure civil servant. This has suggested the conclusion that a small chance of a large payoff is valued higher by many people than by actuaries. The results of an experiment in gambling along these lines, made by Frederick Mosteller at Harvard, are awaited with great interest by economists and statisticians.

able success to govern the world outside himself with science rather than idolatry. And by self-imposed laws for his own social world, he has attemped to set the rules of the game by which he might narrow the gap between winners and losers—or justify it as is—and achieve the higher rating of "social animal," or, as we say in Christianity, the brotherhood of man. So far as achieving any considerable results in this respect, however, man remains a conspicuous failure. Although every man ever born has bowed before the impasse, yet his most lastingly admired works have been efforts to deny the precedence of gambling over reason.

PART TWO

A Theory of Games

LIKE MANY other men, John von Neumann began the study of poker at an early age. He is only forty-six now and he published his first paper on the game in 1928 when he was twenty-three. When the paper appeared, it created a sensation among mathematicians; and ever since then, while von Neumann has achieved so many distinctions in his field, he kept this poker project going until it grew—with the collaboration of Oskar Morgenstern—into a major work on the character of games as models for society.

The first aim of the theory of games is to provide a new mathematical approach to economics, in place of the traditional approach, the mathematical language of which is derived from mechanics. "It is unlikely," the authors say, "that a mere repetition of the tricks that served us so well in physics will do for the social phenomena too." Mathematics essentially is an extension of the traditional discipline of logic. It simply replaced the ordinary literary language of

50

logic with the more complex language of special notation, a device by means of which the range of the human mind—its logic—was increased. In fact, since Newton the development of physics has been made possible by new mathematical tools especially designed for that purpose. The mathematician *qua* mathematician, therefore, is not seeking facts in the ordinary sense, but is engaged in discovering the logical implications of any set of assumptions. The application of mathematics to economics—in contradistinction to its application to physics—has always been up against such a baffling number of unruly facts, in von Neumann's opinion, that life itself, in particular the market, was no place to *begin* the development of mathematical economics. For this, new principles were needed, and principles of mathematics could be established only where assumptions were known. Von Neumann had ideas of this kind when he sat in on a poker game.

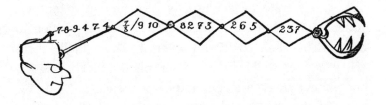

What he saw there was that each player's winnings or losses depended not only upon his own moves but also upon the moves of the others. The poker player could not maximize his gain simply, like a worker on piece rates. To the young mathematician this interdependence appeared identical with the situation encountered in the social economy. The following train of thought went through his mind:

First, no single move of one participant has quality or meaning in itself. It makes sense only as a part of a whole, complete strategy. Not one move therefore but only a complete strategy as such can be assessed rationally. That is, in poker terms, you can analyze a player's strategy only in a whole game or perhaps even in several games.

Second, even a complete strategy of one participant can be judged only on the basis of assumptions or information about the strategies of others. These other strategies cannot be treated as chance events or events controlled merely by probabilities. The "others" must be supposed to be as rational as the participant under consideration, and, of course, they are in precisely the same quandary as he is. Everybody's strategy depends on everybody else's.

Third, this would suggest that all participants be treated together, as a unit—but that, too, is not possible, since they do not co-operate. In fact, usually the main motive for their "interaction" with each other's fate is their opposition to each other—their conflicting interest. Thus, finally there arises the fact, well known in other spheres, that opposition and enmity create a certain interdependence and indivisibility of the opponents' actions, which prohibits treating them as independent individuals, and yet the situation would be most misleadingly described by viewing them as a co-operating unit. This possibility of self-antagonism within an integrated group makes a "vicious circle" and creates the problem of games as well as of social (group) relationship.

The solution—to define rational behavior for the individual, or to say how he is to behave rationally, in the group—has always escaped formulation. Von Neumann saw in the game not only an identity with an aspect of society, but a complete set of workable assumptions—the rules of the game—with which to go to work on the problem of rational behavior. He set out to "win" the game—on paper—regardless of what the opponent did, even though paradoxically the outcome depended in part on what the opponent did.

The only available tool for playing and studying games in the past has been the theory of probability. The theory of probability in fact originated in the study of games of chance, and for such games it is sufficient. It will not do, however, for games of strategy. By separating non-strategical from strategical games, and providing an approach to the latter, the theory of games described here marks a break with classic game theory. This may be seen by looking at the elements of a few well-known games.

The simple one-man game, solitaire, is one man against the cards. It has only chance elements, for one of the players

(the cards, or nature) cannot think and has no influence on the game. All voluntary moves belong to the player who is man. The game therefore is non-strategical and can be played on probability theory alone. The long-run outcome is predictable. Craps and roulette, when played fairly, are likewise non-strategical chance games involving perfect information. Neither the dice nor the wheel is capable of exerting a strategy against the player. One knows exactly what to expect of them in the long run on the basis of probability.

In strategical games, however, the players have a choice of action and their actions are interdependent. Strategical games may also contain either or both of two other elements, namely chance and imperfect information regarding the opponents' strategy. Most strategical games, in fact, contain both chance and imperfect information despite the fact that each is designed to create the same effect: an *uncertainty* for the players to overcome.

The simplest strategical game is matching pennies. It is a rare game, having no chance moves in the rules. The players are confronted only with imperfect information regarding each other's play of heads or tails. If one should be so indiscreet as to play, intentionally or unintentionally, a definite pattern of heads or tails, he might be found out and defeated. Such a method of play would be a strategy, albeit a poor one. The good player therefore voluntarily introduces a chance move (i.e., a random strategy) such as flipping the coin or using some other mechanical device, to avoid knowing his own pattern. With the chances thus set at fifty-fifty, he can in the long run avoid defeat. If his opponent follows the same "rational" approach, the best either can do in this game is break even. It may be worth observing here that if one matched pennies correctly a million times, he could win or lose a thousand pennies. A chance device does not remove the factor of dispersion, the swings of the pendulum of chance. What it removes is a trend.

This game introduces the first important strategical element in the theory of games, namely, random choice; for in this simple game a good player takes risks that depend on chance alone. How one chooses between different risks is one of the questions that has troubled economists as well as game theorists. And to complicate the matter further, one is not alone in taking risks. For one player in judging the value of a definite play must consider the possibility that his opponent will use a chance reply. He must often be able to judge the total value to himself of various chances of winning various amounts.

A THEORY OF GAMES

Matching pennies is the model for a detective story game played by Sherlock Holmes in Conan Doyle's story, *The Final Problem*, once used by Morgenstern as a model of conflicts in life, and played by von Neumann and Morgenstern in the theory of games. Sherlock Holmes, pursued by his murderous enemy, Professor Moriarty, attempts to flee from London to the Continent. He boards the train for Dover. As the train leaves Victoria Station Moriarty arrives on the station platform and the antagonists catch a glimpse of each other. Moriarty, left behind, charters a train and renews the pursuit, a fact of which Holmes is aware. There is one stop between London and Dover, at the town of Canterbury; and it is a rule of this game that if Moriarty catches Holmes he will kill him forthwith. Now each has the choice of getting off at Canterbury or Dover. Which should either do with the greater probability of success? If they meet, they match, as in matching pennies, victory going to Moriarty. If Holmes gets to Dover alone and so escapes there is no match and he wins. But if Holmes gets off at Canterbury and Moriarty goes to Dover, neither gains his objective and they draw. Obviously the stakes are not equal —Holmes having his life to lose, Moriarty only his quarry (and Moriarty may have another opportunity to resume the chase). It is important for Holmes to know what his chances are at either destination; and in fact Conan Doyle endows both his hero and his villain with the required insight, or at any rate the action that that insight would most likely end in. Holmes gets off at Canterbury and Moriarty roars on to Dover.

Here as in matching pennies there is imperfect information and no prescribed chance element. But chance might be introduced by the "players" as a random strategy to give each his best possible outcome. If each assumes the other to be perfectly rational, the solution in the theory of games, categorically stated, is as follows: Assign an arbitrary value of 100 to Moriarty if he "matches" and therefore makes the kill; but only a minus 50 to his loss if Holmes gets to Dover and escapes to the Continent. A computation—the details of which are of no concern here—then says that Moriarty should go to Dover on a 60–40 probability; and Holmes should go to Canterbury on a 60–40 probability. The decision could be made by taking a hundred-card deck of cards, sixty of which are marked Dover and forty Canterbury (vice versa for Holmes), and drawing a card. The chances are then that in one try they will do what Conan Doyle has

them do—although Doyle erred in making the decision a certainty. If Moriarty had used the theory of games, Holmes would have been 48 per cent dead (from a probability standpoint) when he left Victoria Station.

Compare matching pennies with chess. Chess has the strategical elements of choice and interdependence, there are no chance moves, and the information is perfect! Both sources of uncertainty are absent. Each player can see what the other is doing and each knows everything that went before. Only mistakes are possible. Von Neumann says, "If the theory of chess were really fully known there would be nothing left to play." With no chance moves and perfect information there must be either a sure way to win or a sure way to draw. The pleasure in the game arises from the practical difficulty in finding that way through the maze of possible moves and countermoves too numerous even

for the new high-speed calculating machines to handle.*

Bridge and poker have the full complement of game elements: choice, interdependence, imperfect information, and chance. In bridge the chance move is the deal. Imperfect information lies between partners, each of whom has a different position and different information. Bridge in prin-

---

* Norbert Wiener, mathematician, of *Cybernetics* fame (the theory of "control and communication in the animal and the machine," which is associated with the development of high-speed calculating machines), has something to say on the subject of chess: "It is the question whether it is possible to construct a chess-playing machine, and whether this sort of ability represents an essential difference between the potentialities of the machine and the mind. Note that we need not raise the question as to whether it is possible to construct a machine which will play an optimum [rational] game in the sense of von Neumann. Not even the best human brain approximates to this. At the other end, it is unquestionably possible to construct a machine that will play chess in the sense of following the rules of the game, irrespective of the merit of the play. This is essentially no more than the construction of a system of interlocking signals for a railway signal tower. The real problem is intermediate: to construct a machine which shall offer interesting opposition to a player at some one of the many levels at which human chess players find themselves. I think it is possible to construct a relatively crude, but not altogether trivial, apparatus for this purpose. The machine must actually play—at high speed if possible—all its own admissible moves and all the opponent's admissible ripostes for two or three moves ahead."

ciple is a two-man game, each of the two sets of partners acting as a single player. This situation requires the perfecting of information between partners, that is, the perfecting of their organization, by signaling. The rules permit a certain kind of signaling in the bidding, but the signals are not specified in the rules and their use is not mandatory. They are introduced as strategies by the players. The winning bid is an optimum and the subsequent play tests the risks it represents. The hands are played out for the most part on straight probability calculation. Yet there is imperfect information between the opponents too. Misleading plays are sometimes made, as in departures from the usually correct policy for discarding. The decisive aspect of bridge strategy, however, is the clarification of a situation within an organization—getting squared away for the contest with the opponents' organization.

Poker, as suggested earlier, is quite different. Like bridge it has choice, interdependence, imperfect information, and chance. Chance lies in the deal and in the draw if it is a draw game. Otherwise chance plays are a matter of the player's choice. Imperfect information lies between all the players; that is, none presumably knows his opponents' strategies. Each player acts individually and in strategical opposition to the others. The purpose of the basic strategy of bluffing is the opposite of the main strategy of bridge; that is, the signaling is reversed and becomes deception.

The theory of games originated in poker, and that game remains the ideal model of the basic strategical problem. Von Neumann strips the game to its bare structure. He restricts the players to two, the bets to two (high or low) with the alternative of passing, and the raises to one. Like many real poker players, he creates his own variation of the game. The cards are dealt face down but there is no draw. He chooses to call it "stud." The essentials of poker remain: imperfect information concerning the opponent, maintenance of the imperfection by bluffing representations of strength or weakness, the conflict of two maximum intents that can be reconciled only in a bet and a call, after which the outcome is discovered by comparing hands. Each player has the problem of coming to terms with the other player who is unpredictable, even in terms of probabilities, since he, too, can think and plan. The core of the problem then is, how can a player guarantee himself a certain minimum return regardless of the other player's action? This is the problem that has made any action in the market (buyer-seller) or in a contest an irrational gamble, and that by the same token has confounded economic and social theory. The crux of von Neumann's theory lies at this point.

There is imagination but no magic in the theory. It is an act of logic with an unusual twist, which can be followed to the borderline of mathematical computation. At its foundation is the remarkable requirement *that the player assume in advance that he is found out:* that the particular strategy he will follow is already known to his opponent. Such apparent pessimism is antipathetic to the gambling instinct. But it does eliminate one well-known, well-founded anxiety: that if one *is* found out, he will be surprised and defeated. However, this "rational" player prevents both his opponent and to some extent himself from knowing the specific applications of the strategy by making use of random choices. The extent to which this denial and self-denial of information is useful varies from game to game (accounting for it is a feature of the theory of games). Like the penny matcher, who distributes his choices on a random, fifty-fifty basis, the poker player distributes his bluffs irregularly on a controlled-probability basis. He might, for example, choose to bluff 10 per cent of the time, but when these bluffs would occur even he could not tell you.

Now it is von Neumann's contention, which he has

proved mathematically, that if strategy is broadly defined, no loss will be sustained through the "pessimistic" assumption that one's strategy has been found out. For the player who so reconciles himself will, "if he plays well, fare no worse than he would if he 'found out' the opponent's—assuming that the opponent too played well." There's the twist. And it is evident from the assumptions. For the best you can do in strategical competition is to find out your opponent and act accordingly. But if your opponent has acted on the assumption that he is already found out and has randomized his strategy, you gain nothing more by finding him out. Thus you can already see your lowest maximum gain on the average against his best policy: this represents the most you can lose, the least you can gain. For in von Neumann's poker, the highest minimum and the lowest maximum meet at the same point. Von Neumann proved mathematically that this is equally true without exception for all two-person games like his poker (games in which one's losses equal the other's gains). In other words, when playing against a good player, the assumption that one will be found out (to the extent that one may be found out at all) does one no harm. In fact, both players should make this assumption.

The rational player thus does not try to maximize his gain but takes the alternative course of accepting a limitation on the maximum in the form of an "optimum." In declining the "best" possible outcome, he likewise avoids the worst possible outcome. Taking a range of possible high and low gains (or losses), he knows the worst. But to prevent his opponent from finding him out and forcing him to accept the worst, he resorts to chance moves that give him a known probable average outcome. There is no way for his opponent to crack this strategy. For the one who follows it knows where he will come out regardless of what his opponent does.

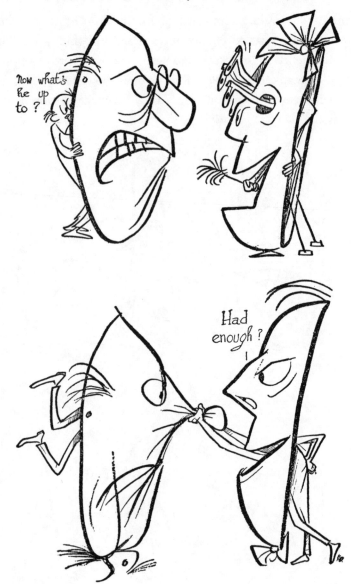

A THEORY OF GAMES

This theory—combining random moves with the pessimistic assumption that one is found out—is called "minimax," meaning the highest minimum, the lowest maximum. It is a theory of the resolution of conflicting maximums in a broad optimum strategy; and as such it is the main pillar of the theory of games.[*]

Minimax

It isn't the "best"....also it isn't the worst and its UNBEATABLE

Dream Stuff (with built in debâcle)

Debâcle

[*] In spite of the "pessimism" in this theory, the player following it can nevertheless secure a result (an expectation value or a statistical mean result) which is no less than that to which the opponent (by similar action) can forcibly limit him. This "value" which both players can unilaterally enforce (one as a minimum, the other as a maximum) is the "value of the game"—if played "correctly." The existence of such a "value" is the decisive mathematical result.

For those who are geometrically minded, the following example, suggested by Jacob Marschak in the *Journal of Political Economy* (April, 1946), may serve. Two persons play a "game" on an altitude map of the United States. One player attempts to get the highest altitude in the latitudinal direction, while the other attempts to get the lowest altitude in the longitudinal direction—the highest and the lowest, respectively, where the two lines of direction intersect. Here then are two conflicting maximums: the highest and the lowest altitude at the same point.

If the first player chooses, say, 40° latitude, the other will choose the longitude corresponding to the Mississippi River. If he chooses 45° latitude the other will choose the longitude of the Great Lakes basin, and so on. However, in the theory of games, the first player should choose a latitude whose lowest altitude is higher than the lowest altitude on any other latitude. In that case, no matter where the second player intersects with his longitudinal line, the first player knows his minimum high. The second player, looking for the lowest altitude, must make a similar move by choosing a longitudinal line whose highest altitude is lower than the highest altitude on any other longitudinal line. Thus he knows his maximum low. Each knows the worst he can do against his opponent's best countermove. The point at which the two lines intersect may not be mutually acceptable to both players, so that if each can see what the other is doing, it may be impossible to determine the outcome. They may keep shifting around to get a better intersection. But if only one player knew where the other was going, he could anticipate his opponent and move to whatever altitude he pleased on his opponent's line and get the best of it. The possibility that one may be found out is the reason why the principle of randomized strategy is introduced into strategical games in which uncertainty exists.

Now, translate this game into poker. "Altitude" becomes expectation of gain; "latitude" and "longitude" become the probability figures which each poker player chooses for randomizing his bluffing to get an average result. On this basis, the two-man poker game always ends for both players at the same point. The long-run outcome is thus determined for each player. Each knows and, being "rational," settles for his highest minimum and lowest maximum expectation. Each has found the optimum, that is, the best strategy in the circumstances.

The theory of "minimax" is a new and important concept in science, and one of the most talked-about novelties in learned circles today. No mathematician has contested its mathematical proofs under the game conditions in which it was constructed. It is the only theory that defines how to proceed rationally in what has classically been considered an irrational situation. It carries the corollary that if your opponent departs from the theory and chooses to act irrationally, you can drive him back to the rational on the pain of losing more in some proportion to his irrationality.

How the minimax strategy protects itself from an opponent's departure from good strategy is demonstrated in poker. Describing the rudiments of the game, von Neumann observes that ". . . a player with a strong hand is likely to make high [bets]—and numerous [raises]—since he has good reason to expect that he will win. Consequently a player who has made a high [bet], or [raise], may be assumed by his opponent—*a posteriori!*—to have a strong hand. This may provide the opponent with a motive for 'Passing.' However, since in the case of 'Passing' the hands are not compared, even a player with a weak hand may occasionally obtain a gain against a stronger opponent by creating the (false) impression of strength by a high [bet], or by [a raise]—thus conceivably inducing his opponent to pass.

"This maneuver is known as 'Bluffing.' It is unquestionably practiced by all experienced players. Whether the above is its real motivation may be doubted; actually a second interpretation is conceivable. That is if a player is known to [bet] high only when his hand is strong, his opponent is likely to pass in such cases. The player will, therefore, not be able to collect on high [bets], or on numerous [raises], in just those cases where his actual strength gives him the opportunity. Hence it is desirable for him to create uncertainty in his opponent's mind as to this correlation— i.e., to make it known that he does occasionally [bet] high on a weak hand.

"To sum up: Of the two possible motives for Bluffing, the first is the desire to give a (false) impression of strength in (real) weakness; the second is the desire to give a (false) impression of weakness in (real) strength. Both are instances of inverted signaling . . . —i.e., of misleading the opponent. It should be observed however that the first type of Bluffing is most successful when it 'succeeds,' i.e., when the opponent actually 'passes,' since this secures the desired gain; while the second is most successful when it 'fails,' i.e., when the opponent 'sees,' since this will convey to him the desired confusing information . . . The possibility of such indirectly motivated—hence apparently irrational—[bets] has also another consequence. Such [bets] are necessarily risky, and therefore it can conceivably be worth while to make them riskier by appropriate countermeasures—thus restricting their use by the opponent."

First of all, the basic good strategy must be always to bet high on a high hand and mostly low on a low hand, "but with occasional irregularly distributed Bluffs." This strategy von Neumann demonstrates to be sound regardless of all but one significant deviation, namely, incorrect bluffing. Any other deviation—for example, betting regularly low on a low hand—will bring losses. But incorrect bluffing against a "correct" player—for example, bluffing more often than is proper on a low hand—brings neither gain nor loss.* By appropriate departures from "correct-

* The poker player who wishes to speculate intuitively might consider the following rule for taking action against a player who is bluffing contrary to good strategy: "if the opponent 'Bluffs' too much for a [given] hand . . . then he can be punished by the following deviations from the good strategy: 'Bluffing' less for hands weaker than [the given hand], and 'Bluffing' more for hands stronger than [the given hand]." The reverse also holds. Thus the defensive counterattack is to imitate your opponent's mistake for stronger hands and to take contrary action for weaker hands.

ness," however, incorrect bluffing can be made a source of losses—while "correct bluffing" is invulnerable to such tactics. This leads to a surprising conclusion regarding poker play: "The importance of 'Bluffing' lies not in the

actual play, played against a good player, but in the pro-
tection which it provides against the opponent's potential
deviations from the good strategy." Anyone who has played
tight poker with strong players knows the validity of this
principle of the primacy of defensive bluffing.

The principle is inherent in the elementary practices of good players playing for substantial stakes, as, for example, in stud, where the first rule is that when you can't beat what you can see, drop; or, again, in draw, where the first rule is don't draw to "shorts" (pairs lower than jacks). Such conservatism of good play precludes bluffing of an aggressive character, except when deliberately intended for effect and preferably at moderate cost. It is, however, necessary to be on the lookout for the opponent's deviation from such proper practices and sometimes to pay well to keep him in line.

In short, von Neumann distinguishes "two varieties of 'Bluffing': an aggressive one practiced by the player who has the initiative and a defensive one—'seeing' irregularly, even with a medium hand, the opponent who is suspected of 'Bluffing.'" Defensive bluffing enforces the minimax strategy. If your opponent leaves it, you win.

Although these are real contributions to poker, von Neumann has not produced the complete poker player. The real game, like the market place, of which it is the model, has many additional complications.

In the two-man poker game the players are unable to reconcile their differences except at a "price" (the bet and the call). The significance of a three-man game is the way it destroys this pure opposition of interest. For this type of game, the authors invent a prototype game with no known counterpart. But any strategical three-man game with similar rules will show the same results.

74

In place of the single situation of pure opposition, three kinds of situation now appear. First, all three players may combine to form a one-man game (against the cards or against nature). Second (if the rules permit), two may combine against one to form a two-person game (with three possible situations of two and one). And third, a pure three-person game with each player on his own. The most important of these three possibilities is the second, the formation of coalitions among the players. A coalition of two playing against one becomes a two-man game, like von Neumann's poker. The two-man game thus is a component of the three-man game. Hence the necessity to understand the two-person game as a prelude to the understanding of the inner workings and outcome of the three-person game. The theory of games shows how coalitions should be formed if there is an advantage in forming them and the rules do not forbid it. Any player, in fact, who fails to attempt a coalition in such circumstances will lose or, more exactly, will gain less. The rational player must make the pessimistic assumption that a coalition may be formed against him; and he must therefore attempt to form one himself. This is significant for the economics of a competitive economy where the "instinct" to combine in the absence of effective preventive rules may be largely a law of survival; that is, not to combine is to risk a loss by a competitor's combination. (Antitrust laws have never been definitive enough to withstand this pressure against them.) In games such reasoning is wholly deductive, and it brings out the full implications of the basic assumptions.

It is remarkable how closely their validity is confirmed by the experience of economic affairs.

An ordinary game model for coalitions, showing in some respects how they form and re-form under changing circumstances, is the card game "Set Back," a variation of pitch, played in the mountains of northwest North Carolina. It is an easier game to follow than von Neumann's mathematical model, and with some adjustments which

will be indicated, it shows the basic idea of coalitions. Set Back is an auction game with bids up to five points (high, low, jack, joker, and a fifth point made by adding up the value of certain cards: ace (4), king (3), queen (2), jack and joker (1), and ten (10)). The deal is six cards to a player with a "widow" of five cards going to the successful bidder. If you get the bid, you declare trumps and proceed to try to take the five points. Failing to make your bid, you are set back the amount of the bid. Eleven points take the game. With three players, one generally gets ahead of the other two, threatening to go out from the vantage point of six or more points. Immediately the other two players give each other tricks to keep them away from the advanced player, and the game is momentarily two against one.

The crucial question for all coalitions then arises: how divide the coalition's gain between the two members? The coalition must give itself tricks, on pain of giving the third player the game; enforcement of the coalition is thus clear and definite. Very soon, however, one of the coalition members, profiting from the arrangement, will himself get six points or more, and threaten to take the game. The first coalition instantly breaks up and the two strong players, fearing each other, give tricks to the weak player to keep them away from each other.

This suggests another unique aspect of coalitions, that under certain conditions weakness is not a complete disadvantage. It does not follow therefore that under all circum-

stances the "fittest" will survive. In economics this principle often takes the form of big organizations allowing or encouraging smaller ones to stay in business to maintain the minimum characteristics of the competitive situation—so as to avoid various dangers of monopoly. In some industries today that are dominated by a few companies it is a custom, almost approaching an ethic, to use kid gloves in competition, and to speak well of one's competitors.

Set Back is an inadequate model from the standpoint of the theory of games. In a true three-man game such as the mathematical model used, there is no sporting rule to prevent a player from offering either of the others a payment to help him get out; since any player may do this, three possible coalitions compete for dominance. In this type of game, it is discovered that the price of remaining in the coalition for any one player must be no less than the cost of defection that the opposed single player could pay

to break the coalition. The result for a three-man majority game is an equipoise of the contending forces brought about by the stress between the possibilities of gain and threats of defection.

The coexistence of flexible and rigid coalitions or rigid refusals to enter coalitions in the market is one of the difficulties which the theory of games has still to overcome. Ethics, language difficulties, and plain inertia prevent many coalitions from forming when the conditions

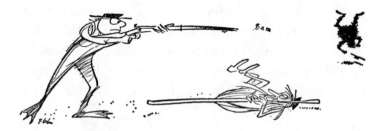

are otherwise favorable. Yet coalitions are a major force in society and, in particular, in industrial markets.

In brief, then, the theory of games says this: Strategical games give a player a choice of action in a situation where all the players are interdependent. Uncertainty in a game may derive merely from a practical limitation on foresight, as in chess. But more often it derives from a chance element (controllable by the theory of probability) and from imperfect information on the part of one player regarding what his opponents may do (uncontrollable except in the theory of games). Strategy is a policy devised to reduce and control these uncertainties. Strategy may require the introduction of chance moves by the players to prevent their pattern of play from being discovered, that is, to increase the imperfection of information. Good strategy requires the use of the principle of "minimax," that is, a policy in which a range of possible high and low gains is adopted on the assumption that one might be found out. But to avoid being found out one obscures the specific pattern of play by randomizing the strategy with chance plays. Average (statistical) results—rather than the high·

or the low—are thus obtained regardless of what the opponent does. If both players in a two-person game in which one's losses are equal to the other's gains follow this policy, they will, theoretically, arrive at the "value of the game." If the game is "symmetrical," having equal conditions on both sides, the value of the game will be zero, i.e., the players

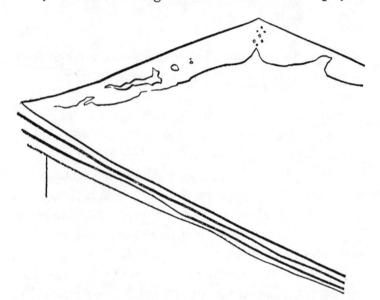

break even. But if one player is irrational (tries to maximize his gain), the rational player, theoretically, will win.

The rational policy is the best policy that can be tried by either player, even though on individual plays one may lose. And the long-run results are the best that can be obtained even though the pendulum of chance may vary the results at any given time. In the three-and-more-person games, coalitions, if allowed, must be attempted, for there is a gain to be made in combination. This brings the three-person game back to a two-person game (two *vs.* one), with this difference: that this two-person game is under pressure from the third player, who must attempt to break up the combination and form one of his own with one of the other players. This complication continues in the four-person game (two *vs.* two, or three *vs.* one), and so on as more persons enter the game. And finally, these circumstances, and the best strategy for them, are identical in economic life. The same may be said for military, political, and other games.

PART THREE

The "Game" of Business

THE CORE of business is the market. The core of the market is the relationship of buyer and seller, whether either is an individual or a corporation. The theory of games investigates the interior of this relationship with the game models just described.

Buyer and seller are the same as the players in a two-man poker game. Each tries to "maximize" his gain and in the market, of course, both may gain; for each gets rid of something of which he has a relative excess and obtains something of which he is relatively short. But the degree of economic gain is always at stake in the strategical problem of arriving at a price. The seller cannot maximize his gain pure and simple, for he must relate his asking price to an expectation concerning the buyer. Likewise the buyer cannot maximize his gain except by getting the goods for nothing. He bids according to an expectation concerning the seller. Each must take the other fellow's thoughts into account. The opposition between bid and ask is resolved in a price that represents not a maximum but a resolution of conflicting (maximum) desires in what each hopes is his optimum. All buyers and sellers have intuitive exchange policies, or strategies, for arriving at such optimums. They are the supreme talent of the businessman—from the street vendor to the corporation manager.

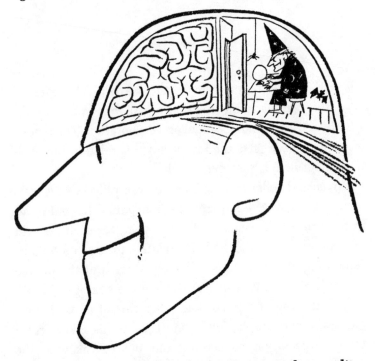

In one sense this is self-evident. It corresponds to reality. Yet it has always confounded economists in their efforts to describe economic activity. No conventional formula

is able to explain, for example, how the price of manu-
factured goods is arrived at, or the cause of combinations,
which are typical of industry.

Only in the past twenty years has modern economic
theory generally recognized "monopolistic competition"
and "oligopoly" (i.e., few sellers) as central to the competitive economic system—rather than as a discrepancy
in the concept of pure competition. Classical economics
makes its calculations on the assumption that no single
individual produces a large enough amount of the total
supply to effect a relevant price change. Price, accordingly,
is the automatic regulator of supply and demand. This
situation may be known to the farmer, but it is rarely
known to the manufacturer. For when only a few traders
(the characteristic Big Three or Big Four) are present in
a market each has some degree of control over output and
price. Monopoly influence in this sense is characteristic
of industrial markets. Free competition among many individuals has been steadily displaced by the strategical competition and struggle of smaller numbers of combinations
of individuals in such forms as corporations, trade unions,
and various associations.

The theory of games approaches economic life from the
standpoint of the individual (one person or one unit). It
is microscopic in contrast to the three historic macroscopic
systems of Smith (explicit among his followers), Marx,
and Keynes, and as far from them as nuclear physics is
from astronomy. Somewhere in economic thought the

macroscopic and microscopic approaches may meet, as astronomy and earth-bound physics did in Isaac Newton. Adam Smith, the "father" of capitalism, never knew the Industrial Revolution nor saw the hand of man at market controls. He believed simply that in "natural liberty" the "invisible hand" would guide the economy to the most efficient employment of resources. From this his followers constructed the theory of pure competition, which remained forever a fiction. Karl Marx's vast, melancholy synthesis of political, social, and economic forces in the theory of classes moved everything from accumulated capital to wars and revolutions in half-disciplined, half-prophetic sweeps leading both naturally and by intervention to the socialist organization of society: a theory that has come to be accepted more readily on faith than by observation and analysis. John Maynard Keynes in his major work, *The General Theory of Employment, Interest and Money,* in 1936 made the most recent, heroic effort to cope with economic life on the basis of such aggregates as national income, consumption, savings, and investment. Keynes rested his case on an equilibrium of aggregates (e.g., income equals consumption plus investment), but to protect the equilibrium at a high level against the dynamic "stagnation" of capital (similar to Marx's "falling rate of profit"), manipulation of at least one variable was required (such as Roosevelt's fiscal policies, particularly those relating to expenditure). That is as close as Keynesian economics comes to the integration of economics with political economy. Among the things it does not explain

Karl Marx

are the strategical combinations that are formed at every level of the economy for the purpose, in part, of manipulating aggregates.

Although much good descriptive work has been done in economic thought, yet no system has a real claim on being a universal theory accounting for the major economic phenomena and capable of prediction. Like other social sciences, economics speaks not of probabilities but of likelihoods, and there is not much agreement on them. Quite apart from the vagaries of nature, neither the individual nor society can be sure whether prosperity or depression lies ahead, nor whether the most reasonable effort is being made to use the resources at hand. The mystery lies in man's relation to man.

The authors of the theory of games, however, are not the first to examine individual economic behavior. Many economists, the "marginalists," for example, make efforts to understand the subjective basis of individual behavior but do not pursue the individual far into his social life. They find, plausibly, that each additional unit of any good brings a person less satisfaction than the preceding unit. This is almost if not exactly physiological—each glass of milk that one drinks in succession, for example, presumably removes less hunger than the previous one. But the "marginalists" do not examine strategical market relationships (e.g., "shopping") within which the anticipated event is valued. They have generally assumed, rather, that each person independently seeks his maximum satisfaction. Game theory shows that that is not what happens. People may pursue maximums, but they will probably come out with some limitation, that is, an optimum.*

* The "marginal theory of value" modified and substantially displaced in dominant economic thought the "labor theory of value" which was originated by the celebrated economist, David Ricardo, and adopted by

The theory of games, which is objective, is meeting opposition from those "marginalists" who believe that utility (the capacity of goods to satisfy desires) can be ordered but not measured. The authors of the theory of

Marx as his basic theory of exploitation. According to this theory, labor is the true source of all value. Marx (who substituted power to labor for labor) tried to make the theory stick by proving the existence of a net product above subsistence, which was divided into wages, profit and rent (for Ricardo the net was all in rent). According to Marx, the profit and rent are in effect stolen from the workers and become "surplus value." The labor theory of value, however, was not plausible if labor were not the only or main means of production. And it was unable to account for the market value of unique, non-reproducible rarities such as, say, a Leonardo da Vinci painting. The discrepancy was not minor, for very few industrial products are undifferentiated (a Da Vinci is only a special case—the absolute differentiation). The "marginal" theory has never been completely satisfactory either, and the theory of games by shooting at its "maximum" fallacy may be its Nemesis.

games assert that if your preferences are consistent and in a sense orderly, then, for you, utility can be expressed numerically. This need not be in terms of money (does $5 mean the same thing to a man with $5, another with $5,000, and another with $50,000?). The mathematician also assumes, for example, that the utility of a 10 per cent chance of getting a Lincoln and a 90 per cent chance of getting a Chevrolet has a definite combined value that can be compared with the certainty of getting a DeSoto or Chrysler. In military applications it is said that the question is not how much you gain on the average but rather how often you win. The mathematician would reply simply that someone wants a very large value given to the difference between winning and losing. If all the players in a game play for money alone, the theory applies most simply since "valuation" in dollars is formally easier.

From the standpoint of the individual there are three possible economic situations on earth: one man alone, two men, or three or more men. One man is Robinson Crusoe alone on an island. He plays there the game of solitaire, maximizing his gain uncomplicated by anything but the forces of nature, which are predictable, at least in such terms as probable rainfall and the probability of a tornado. Robinson Crusoe is also theoretically pure communism in which the distribution of wealth is fixed by definition and society proceeds as one against nature. (As we know, Stalin's particular kind of "Communism" requires a considerable coercion to maintain a semblance of fixity.)

If there are two men on earth, the individual enters into the relation of exchange (buyer-seller), in which the problem of the other fellow appears; he can no longer maximize his gain but must seek a limitation of the possibilities in an optimum. But if there are three men, the novelty occurs that two of them may gain more by combining against the third (e.g., two sellers against a buyer, or vice versa). These three situations are the same as those found in games.

Von Neumann and Morgenstern approached the problem of the economic individual with simple game models because science always begins with simple models. In games, strategies are simple, observable, and susceptible of abstraction. Games themselves are sets of rules, abstractly comparable to physical conditions of economic life. A rule of a game, for example, is that one card is higher than another. This is equivalent to a physical fact like, for example, the existence of transportation, or the durability or perishability of a product. Around these physical and chemical rules—which cannot be violated —strategies are exercised. In the theory of games, the influence of custom, prejudice, and the like on the formation of coalitions is studied as complicating "standards of behavior." *

Unlike economics, games are non-productive, but that is no obstacle to a mathematician: his games may have the device of a fictitious player who must supply the real players with their gains from productivity. Ordinary games are less complicated than the market, but mathematicians contend that they manage to work with games that are infinitely complex. The real difficulty with the market— from the standpoint of constructing economic theory—is not so much its complexity but the fact that one does not know the exact rules. If the rules were known to the last comma, it would be a "game."

Any industry serves as an example of strategical game

* The whole "ethical system" that underlies a society or the whole "social order," is a "standard of behavior" in the theory of games. In a game played by three or more persons, this "standard of behavior" itself represents a "solution." The actual conduct of an individual within the established order is a strategy; and any one of the many actual and possible distributions of positions and benefits that conform with the principles of the established order is an element belonging to that "solution."

play. Take the liquor industry, which like steel, oil or automobiles has only a few sellers. The following story was told at length in the September, 1948, issue of *Fortune* magazine. Samuel Bronfman of Seagram had come down from Canada at the time of repeal and built his organization on blended whiskey in the tradition of Canadian and Scotch whiskeys. U.S. distillers, slow to adopt blends, preferred to sell the traditional American rye and bourbon. But blended whiskey could be nationally advertised to better advantage (rye and bourbon being largely regional); and Bronfman made the most of it. His marketing strategy consisted of blends, brand names and mild taste. Eventually there was a contest for leadership in the industry between Seagram and Schenley. Lewis Rosenstiel of Schenley, an old-school U.S. distiller, divided his attention between blends and straights. Now whiskey is made at one time to be sold four or more years later, and there is a corresponding risk in the inventory. Keep too little and you may run short. Keep too much and you may get stuck (whiskey consumption roughly follows the income curve; and as in any industry total inventories can get out of hand, resulting, in the absence of mandatory fair trade laws, in occasional price wars). "Holidays" during World War II had eliminated several crops of whiskey and inventories generally were low. Rosenstiel is known as an inventory strategist. He came out of the war period with brand sales off but with perhaps half of the remaining aged whiskey inventory in the U.S. Bronfman of Seagram had used up a large part of his whiskey inventory in gain-ing record brand sales. In this situation, they had a contest for the leadership, a kind of two-man game within the industry.

Facing a forthcoming shortage, Bronfman could either buy scarce bulk whiskey at a losing price and maintain Seagram's brand sales with a decline in profits, or maintain his rate of profit out of his remaining inventory with a decline in brand sales—or follow a mixed policy. In any event he could not maximize both brand sales and profits. Rosenstiel could sell the inventory to Bronfman at high bulk prices and no sales cost and thus maximize profits in the immediate circumstance; or he could put the inventory into Schenley brands with an expensive and risky sales campaign to raise brand sales at less profit. Like Bronfman, but for different reasons, he could not maximize both brand sales and profits.

Nor could the policies of the antagonists fail to conflict; for Rosenstiel, who, having the better inventory, had the dominant choice, could reconcile their difference only by taking profit and giving Bronfman the market (brand sales), i.e., take short-term gains at the cost of long-term losses. Within limits, Bronfman would have been glad to buy the market (take short-term losses with long-term gains)—if Rosenstiel would let him. But Rosenstiel wouldn't. Each sought an optimum move on a strategical basis. The game broadened out with larger numbers as Bronfman got some whiskey from another source. Rosenstiel opened a "back-label" campaign to make his aged stocks pay off. The consequences of the struggle have not been told, but whatever they are, they are the consequences of conscious strategy. Theoretically, Seagram and Schenley had another alternative, namely, to combine. There are good reasons why they would not, yet each of these corporate individuals like so many others in industry had grown large through combination.

Two-man games appear also in political economy. The situation in the duel, mentioned in the Introduction—with its problem, when to shoot—is suggestive of a major problem in fiscal policy: when should the Federal Reserve System take deflationary measures and when inflationary measures? Not too early and not too late, and not without considering their interdependence. If the theory of games had the computational wherewithal and a sufficient description of economic facts, it could solve this problem (i.e., determine the optimum, "minimax" fiscal moves) as in the duel, or two-man poker: the forces of inflation *vs.* the forces of deflation. As it is, fiscal policy makers should try to play it intuitively in the same way, and probably often do.

A similar problem lies in government grain-buying policy. Government purchases are large enough to affect commodity prices. The object of buying policy is to avoid driving prices up too far. Purchases therefore are often made on a "down swing," when there is such a movement. The timing of government purchases thus is tied to the movement of the open market price. But that price (for "free" grain and for grain sold above price supports) is made by grain traders on competitive bidding in the futures markets. Traders naturally build into the price their calculations regarding future government buying policy. Government buyer and grain trader thus find themselves in a strategical game, the policy of each including an anticipation of the policy of the other.

The three-man coalition game can be played as an auction with one seller and two buyers. The seller has a reserve price of, say, $10 on the object to be sold. The first buyer is willing to go to not more than $15; the second buyer to not more than $20. Clearly the second buyer being the stronger will get the object. Ordinarily he is expected to get it for something over $15. But suppose the second buyer approaches the first and makes a deal to eliminate competitive bidding. He can then get the object for something over $10. The deal, however, requires a division of the spoils. The second, stronger buyer must pay the first, weaker buyer something for making the coalition. That payment must be enough to yield the second buyer the "best" profit, and yet enough to ensure that his partner will remain in the coalition: two maximums which must be resolved. For another, rival deal is possible—in game theory but not in classical economics—namely this: The seller may cross the market and break up the coalition by paying something to the second buyer to restore the bidding and thereby push the selling price back above

$15. Thus each two-man game in this three-man game is under the influence of the other possible two-man games, in arriving at the distribution payment.

In the theory of games a number of solutions, i.e., distribution schemes, are possible, some of which are enforceable and therefore dominate others. In classical theory the weaker buyer gets nothing; in game theory he gets a bribe, and the bribe will be expressed in the price. Here the difference between classical economics and game theory can be shown with simple numbers. In classical theory the price is between $15 and $20 (all going to the seller). In game theory it is between $10 and $20, depending on the bargaining ability of the players.

The basic strategy of organizers of industry from the beginning has been to substitute combination for large-number competition. The value which J. P. Morgan put on combination was indicated in the capitalization of the United States Steel Corporation in 1901. The Corporation, which brought together about 65% of the steel capacity of the United States, was capitalized at about twice the tangible value given to its separate properties before combination. The specific combinative value (about three-quarters of a billion dollars minus an unknown value put on "good will") was expressed in the new common stock—attacked as "watered stock"—which eventually paid off as the technical and strategical market advantages of combination were realized. The Corporation later met rivalry from other combinations which were organized in opposition to it.

Rockefeller's genius similarly expressed itself in combinations. But some of these early combinations, as they were organized, were unwieldy. Standard Oil stockholders probably benefited from the trust's court-ordered dissolution in 1911. It became impolitic thereafter, under the Sherman Act, for one organization to hold an overwhelming share of the market. For that reason or because its ability to compete against counter-combinations was injured by organizational and management defects, the Steel Corporation retreated to its present holdings of about one-third of the industry's ingot capacity. Its present leadership of the industry is maintained by modern market techniques described in oligopoly and game theory.

THE "GAME" OF BUSINESS

No effort has been made to apply game theory rigorously to actual market situations. It is the opinion of the mathematicians who created it that social science has to proceed, like physical science, without the criterion of usefulness. On the assumption of the identity of games and economics, the theory requires development in handling more and more complicated games with larger numbers of players. Game theory thus will make its discoveries through its models. It will not prevent the next depression, nor is it likely that any other presently known theory will either. It is risky therefore to try to anticipate how game theory will work out; but here is a suggestion of what it might look like in the field of antitrust policy.

Since industry supplanted agriculture as the dominant form of Western economy, monopoly has been an absorbing and confounding problem in politics and economics. In political economy, it appears often as the problem of the size and number of firms required to make up the checks and balances of political democracy. In market economy it appears as the more restricted problem of the relationships and behavior of buyers and sellers in the market. Classical theory, as suggested earlier, assumes the existence of large numbers of buyers and sellers, each without appreciable individual influence on price. In reality industrial competition is characteristically among relatively small numbers, each with some influence on output and price—and some influence on demand too, since demand is a function of price.

The price set by one seller will usually be met by another. Price wars resolve the issue too soon and too strongly for most businessmen. Other methods of competition are pursued: changes in the quality and appearance of goods, salesmanship, services, advertising, inventory and capacity manipulations, integration, new products and processes, and so on, each move of this kind having a bearing on the move of another. The question whether this welter of interdependent activity between small numbers of (often large) firms is strictly competitive is given at least three answers: yes, no, and yes-and-no, depending upon what aspect of the market is considered paramount.

It is possible to look at the market alternatively in terms of its "structure" or "performance": the elements of structure consisting mainly of the number of firms, their relative sizes, collusion, and the situation with regard to the entrance of a newcomer; the elements of performance consisting mainly of output, cost, price, and new products and processes. How judgments about competition and monopoly depend upon the weight given to one or the other of these sets of standards is revealed in the contrasting points of view taken by two eminent economists, Friedrich Hayek (*The Road to Serfdom*, University of Chicago Press, 1945) and J. A. Schumpeter (*Capitalism, Socialism and Democracy*, Harper & Brothers, 1947). Hayek says, "The price system will fulfill [its] function only if competition prevails, that is, if the individual producer has to adapt himself to price changes and cannot control them." This is the apparently utopian assumption of the classical theory of pure competition; it relies upon the assumption of a structure of large numbers, and would probably require the complete dismantling of modern industry. Schumpeter, on the other hand, says, "The fundamental impulse that sets the capitalist engine in motion comes from the new consumers' goods, the new methods of production or transportation, the new markets, the new forms of industrial organization that capitalist enterprise creates. . . ." Schumpeter, however, concludes that the capitalist, by his good performance, is destroying the economic and cultural institutions of capitalist society from within and is thereby unwittingly, unwillingly but inevitably creating socialism.

Between these extremes of reliance respectively on structure and performance are the "realists" who have undertaken to develop a quasi-political theory of "workable" or "effective competition." Yet this school is itself divided between those who accent one or the other set of standards. The young economist M. A. Adelman of M.I.T. explains his preference for the tests of performance in the form of a parable which may bring this digression back to the theory of games.

"Let us imagine a store being newly started in a town or neighborhood previously without one. The owner is a local monopolist, protected, but not completely, by the distance to his nearest rival. His profits attract a new store into the area, and the market divides between them. For each one, the cost of doing additional business would be very low: they have excess capacity. There is a constant temptation to cut prices toward this low cost of additional business ('incremental cost') . . . But open price cuts are futile, for they will be matched within the hour—the net result being merely lower profits for both. Customers are not price conscious, anyway. Better to offer additional services, which quickly gain attention, to offer more premiums, and to advertise more. As both do so (while also trying to make a few large sales at special prices), costs rise, and margins and prices are raised to cover them. There is no agreement; it is the normal thing to do. As prices rise, sales decline and excess capacity grows. More services and advertising shift the burden back and forth, increasing it all the while. The temptation to cut prices grows, but the higher the cost structure the more disastrous this can be. Thus two completely independent business firms are not conspiring; they desire only a fair profit and are probably earning less. Nevertheless, they are exploiting consumers by making them pay for the upkeep of twice the capacity they need and twice the owners. Finally some low ruffian, in search not of a reasonable but of a large profit, opens a supermarket near by, engages in strenuous price competition, and puts them both out of business —but not before they have had time to complain bitterly that he is 'unfair,' to importune the legislature to stop his 'selling below cost' (their cost, not his), and all the rest of it.

"This is, in microcosm, the rise and decline of oligopoly heaven. Its keynotes, and essential features, are not size, or agreement, but restricted output, higher prices and excess capacity. Effective competition would exclude them." * Edward S. Mason of Harvard, an authority on antitrust problems, however, concludes "these tests [structure and performance] must be used to complement rather than to exclude each other." But Mason has his fingers crossed so far as getting a definite result is concerned. The standard is still double and the correlation will in the end be made according to the predisposition of the judge.

Now for the hazard. How would Adelman's parable look as a game? There are four players: the two cost-plus grocers, the supermarket and the consumer. The two grocers make a coalition against the consumer; they play a two-man game with each other which results in taking more money from the consumer. Along comes the supermarket offering prizes or payments to the consumer in the form of lower prices (based on higher output and lower costs). Supermarket and consumer make a coalition (called a "convention" in standard economic terminology) against the grocer coalition. The supermarket receives payments in profits (from larger volume at lower prices for each consumer); the consumer receives payments in savings. But the game is not over when the first grocer coalition retires from the field. If the supermarket has other competitors, as it usually does, the consumer can maintain a strong position by threatening coalitions with those competitors. But if the supermarket and its competitors now combine, they could make additional gains through higher

* *Harvard Law Review,* September, 1948.

prices for a while at the consumer's expense. The situation with which the game began would then be restored, to be upset, perhaps, by another newcomer.

If the supermarket, however, had no easily reachable competitors, it would achieve the position of a single-firm monopoly, from which it could dominate the consumer in the two-man game, and until this was threatened or upset it could be expected that prices would rise. Monopoly in that case would be checked and controlled only by the non-existent but latent competition inherent in the invitation of high prices. Thus the problem of "structure" (numbers, sizes and their relationships) returns. In the language of games, "structure" becomes the strategical position and interdependent relationship of the players. Performance becomes the payments made in strategical play. The dualism of structure and performance are thus integrated into the single concept of a game.

In the United States, the game has a fifth player, the government (Congress, Antitrust Division, Federal Trade Commission and the courts). The government gets into the game mainly by way of the Sherman Act and its complement of related acts, banning "conspiracy" and "monopoly." Businessmen often, perhaps usually, view the Sherman Act as an unavoidable risk. For the Act is vague, and timidity on the part of one person or firm, regarding the uncertain legality of a proposed action, may be met with daring of another. Paradoxically, to survive in competition one has to risk the penalty of being monopolistic. The acceptance or rejection of such risks is a matter of strategy. Game theory thus suggests that antitrust policy itself should be viewed as a strategy.

In the absence of a widespread ethical attitude among businessmen toward the Sherman Act, the "game" (businessmen *vs.* antitrust agencies) might be played to achieve optimum results. Businessmen—or more often their public representatives—often complain that they do not know the "rules"; and in fact there is considerable inconsistency in the interpretation of antitrust regulations. These inconsistencies, however, are in part of a historical kind, reflecting the shifts of political power as well as the gradual development of more realistic economic doctrine. They also reflect the opportunism of law which encourages prosecutors to sue first and make inquiries on a policy level afterward. It would be impossible, since neither the businessman nor the economist knows all the physical rules by which business proceeds, to frame precise and detailed antitrust regulations. The vagueness of the Sherman Act is in good part a reflection of the vagueness of the economic circumstances. Enforcement agencies, for their part, at best are able to give only a limited coverage to the economic scene. Complete coverage would be impractical from the standpoint of cost. It would seem then that if the various agencies of government could provide a reasonably consistent interpretation for a period of time, and if the prosecution agencies followed a broad strategical policy, including perhaps, when suitable, a chance method of

selecting cases, businessmen might be able to put a somewhat clearer risk value on their actions. This might result
at least in enough differences of opinion to keep a substantial and perhaps decisive number of them out of the
twilight areas. This might constitute an optimum antitrust
policy.

The importance of the three-person coalition game for
economics is its dissection of the phenomenon of "oligopoly" and "monopolistic competition," which has long
baffled economic thought. Unlike any others, von Neumann
and Morgenstern build coalitions integrally into their
theory. The complications that one extra player adds to
game solutions, however, are both good and bad for the
theory of games. For although the extra player reveals the
law of coalitions, by the same token he shows the fantastic
complications involved in extending actual mathematical
computations to situations involving large numbers. Even in
a ten-person game, the players can be split into two opposing coalitions in 511 different ways. If the coalitions crystal-
lize gradually from subcoalitions (with as many hierarchic
interstages as necessary), the number of possible structures
is still larger.

It is by no means inevitable, however, that such multitu-
dinous combinations come into existence. The trade-union
movement shows how large numbers of economic individuals can group themselves back into small numbers of
strategy-minded units. Yet the problem of large numbers is

the greatest challenge the theory of games has to meet. In its present form also, the theory of games is avowedly static, i.e., it does not deal with change. These two problems have been raised as objections to the theory. To von Neumann and Morgenstern they are not valid objections, but limitations in the present stage of the theory's development. In fact, the concepts static and dynamic are so misty that the authors may be too modest in affirming the static limitation. However, if the theory is ever able to cope dynamically with large numbers, it will have reached the ideal scientific goal of prediction. At present it is close to prediction only in military games.

Large numbers of course do not bother mathematicians. In physical science the theory of gases, involving unbelievably large numbers of molecules, is an exact science just because of the large numbers. This has suggested that ideal free competition might be the truly calculable situation, the most predictable circumstance in which free enterprise could find itself. This conclusion parallels Adam Smith's implied assumption that large numbers of individuals, each pursuing his own interests, would on the whole bring about the best or most efficient employment of resources. It is an attractive if utopian thought, as revolutionary in its way as pure communism. For the present type of "monopolistic competition" the theory might answer the question whether the optimum profit is identical with optimum production, and whether this is identical with optimum social and individual well-being. It would be interesting to know whether pure or monopolistic competition produces the fuller employment of resources. The theory of games makes no promises. But it finds man, not inanimate nature, making the decisions, and studies them.

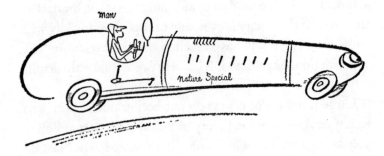

PART FOUR

Military and Other Games

THE THEORY of games was designed specifically as an economic theory, but it has displayed a power of generality in its impact on other social disciplines. Its three principal novelties—randomized strategy,

optimum (minimax) strategy,

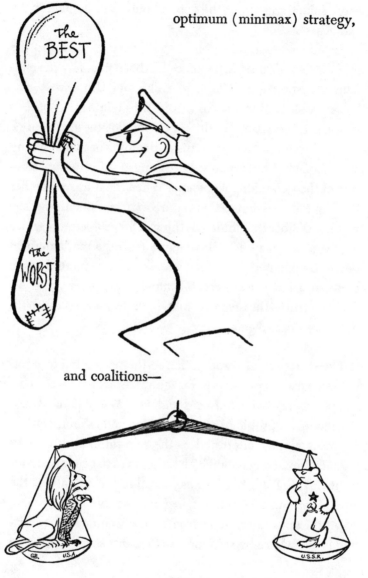

and coalitions—

show something about the general nature of conflict in social organization.

An advanced application of the theory of games to the foundations of statistical science has been made by the eminent statistician, A. Wald, of Columbia University. The basic problem of statistical theory is to relate a hypothesis to some information. If there is a conflict the problem is, which is wrong, the hypothesis or the information? Making a decision here corresponds to arriving at the optimum solution of the two-man poker game. When the information lies in nature, it is assumed that nature may be difficult but she will not deliberately hide anything. The problem therefore is solved in a man *vs.* nature game (using a mathematical device by which the one-man game can be converted into a two-man game). But in social statistics people may lie. To find the truth, the scientist may have to lie too, and both play a strategical game.

The strategies of co-operation in the perfecting of information between partners in bridge are discussed by Herbert A. Simon (*Administrative Behavior*, Macmillan, 1948), as a model for problems of organization and administration. Simon is mainly interested in the non-rational aspects of organizational behavior which he believes to be more significant in this field, but he has something to say about the kind of rational action found in game theory:

"At the opposite extreme from a purely competitive situation is one where two or more participants share a common goal, and where each has sufficient information as to what the others are going to do to enable him to make correct decisions. This is precisely what is meant by 'teamwork.' The purpose of signals in football, or bidding in bridge, is to enable each player in a team to form accurate expectations as to what his teammates are going to do, so that he can determine the proper means for cooperating with them to reach the common aim . . .

"If the activity is competitive, then, it may exhibit a certain instability . . . But this same instability may result even if the activity is cooperative, provided the participants are insufficiently informed." The theory of games suggests that it takes a strategy to become informed.

Political strategists often attempt to explain everything that a powerful nation says in the United Nations or does on the political scene in terms solely of a definite strategical pattern which it is assumed can be discovered by fitting all the pieces together. Such analysis fails to account for the possibility that some political moves may be made on a random basis just in order to throw the opposition off the scent. A "rational" political leader, according to game theory, ought to make such random moves. The political game is closer to matching pennies in this respect than it is to chess; closer to poker in its bluffing moves; closer to bridge in some of its inner-organization cleanups; and closer to the three-person game in the forming of alliances. Since all of these strategical elements are contained in the three (and more) person game, it is the model for the "game" of politics.

Politics, in fact, is a combinative art. The political conventions of the Republican and Democratic parties, for example, are coalition games. Each candidate goes in generally with a number of votes short of a nominating majority. The "game" is for each candidate to attempt to secure that majority through coalitions with other-candidate groups and at the same time to break up or prevent competing coalitions. Such coalitions have a political "price" in the form of patronage or policy. The price paid by any member of a coalition is determined by how well he would fare in case of a defection. Unless one candidate has done all the work in advance and comes in dominant, as Roosevelt did on the occasion of each renomination, the political convention is invariably at least a three-man game. For when there are two strong candidates there is always the unknown but very real dark horse who may have a better chance due to the

possibility of the strong candidates being unwilling to join forces and therefore canceling each other out. Stability in this basically unstable situation is obtained for a time by the leading candidate; as he pushes forward, delegates get on the band wagon for fear of being left out of the pay-off. If the stronger oppositions are able to hold out and stop the advance, no matter how close it may be to victory, the band-wagon coalition will collapse, and a new leader will make a run for it with the same coalition technique.

Stalin's career is a lesson in coalition strategy. Take three spectacular and consequential episodes on different political levels. First, after Lenin died in 1924 there followed a long period of internal political maneuvers in the Bolshevik party. The "triumvirate" of Zinoviev, Kamenev and Stalin opposed Trotsky. When Trotsky's party position was weakened, the "triumvirate" dissolved. Stalin formed a new coalition with Bukharin (including also Rykov and Tomsky), and this group opposed Trotsky on the one hand and the combination of Zinoviev and Kamenev on the other. After various moves and countermoves in the course of which Zinoviev and Kamenev were weakened, the latter uncertainly joined with their former opponent, Trotsky. The issue of power thus was drawn between two combinations. According to the Bolshevik rules no holds were barred. Few ethical or other rigidities complicated the game, unless they were represented by Trotsky's inhibitions. Nothing was needed more by these men than a little game theory, and only one had it. Here in schematic outline is what appears to have happened:

117

From 1921, the New Economic Policy, favoring a certain amount of private enterprise, had been functioning in Russia. Trotsky, the "leftist," was for an early turn to high-speed industrialization and collectivization. Bukharin, the "rightist," fearing the political consequences of rapid collectivization, stood for a more gradual change of economic policy (and there were other disagreements). Whether policy or party power was the stronger motive is a moot point. It appears, however, that Stalin did not forcefully represent a policy here. His forte as "secretary" had been organization, that is, the establishing of the inner-party bureaucratic pay-offs. Bukharin and Stalin (with others) had the power to eliminate Trotsky from the scene and the immediate game, and did so in 1927. Trotsky for his part appears to have made no serious effort to prevent this coalition or to break it up by offering a price that would break it up, or at any rate, make it insecure. The expulsion of Trotsky was fatal to Bukharin. For Stalin and Bukharin then immediately went into a struggle. In this two-man game, Stalin, a minority interest when Trotsky was present, found himself, perhaps not to his surprise, in the dominating position. Bukharin was forthwith disposed of. Stalin pursued the policy of rapid industrialization and collectivization (Five Year Plan). In the next few years all real or potential challengers were physically eliminated. This was the denouement of the inner Bolshevik struggle, ending in the "stability" of Stalinist absolutism.

The next episode took place in 1932 as Hitler approached power in Germany. In Germany there was a three-man game in progress between the Socialists, Communists, and Fascists. None had a majority. Any coalition would win. The Socialists lacked a coalition policy and opposed more or less equally both Communists and Fascists. Stalin, in control of the Communists, forbade an alliance with the Socialists; this took the form of an official theory of "social fascism," according to which the Socialists were the greater enemy. Stalin, in other words, declared a negative coalition with the Fascists against the Socialists. Apparently he wished to obtain a monopoly of the German left and to play out a two-man game against Hitler; and the negative coalition enabled him to use Fascist as well as Communist power to destroy the Socialists. Hitler was willing. He got the Chancellorship from Hindenburg and went in and cut down both oppositions. The two-man game between the Communists and Fascists failed to materialize within Germany.

The third episode is familiar. The historic British "balance of power" policy, which was intended to prevent a coalition between France and Germany, dwindled—in the presence of Soviet Russia and Fascist Germany—to a "policy" of indecision. Several big nations jockeyed for international coalition positions throughout the thirties. Stalin went with Hitler in 1939. Hitler made his defection in 1941, and Stalin came together with the Allies. During the past war certain concessions to Stalin made by Roosevelt and Churchill were defended on the ground that they were necessary to maintain the coalition, that is, to prevent Stalin's defection from the Allies. The assumption was that

119

alternative solutions existed for Stalin and that continuous payments to him were required to maintain the stability of the coalition against the Axis.

Since the war, the combinative nature of society appears to be resolving world politics into a two-man game. Each side is engaged in clarifying its inner organization—albeit on different ethical, social, and political principles—and in conducting its outer struggle in a cold-war duel. Yet not every player on the world scene is committed, so that the three-or-more-person game remains the model of international affairs.

Some games end in revolutions, from which something may be learned. Any income distribution is under attack in society. Revolutions are based in good part upon organizing

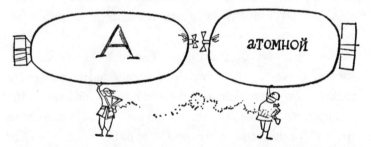

and extending existing social hostilities on the model of another and "different" distribution. Yet societies with inequitable distribution, dissatisfaction, and inner conflict show stability for long periods of time. Game theory models indicate that an inequitable organization is protected by a kind of similarity of alternative arrangements. A coalition cannot be broken except by a vastly different distribution, which is difficult to devise. If the "revolutionaries" find a situation in which their proposals can prevail, they immediately come under attack, and once the revolution is in motion, it is difficult to make it stable, that is, to find a distribution that can no longer be upset. All distributions become unstable as competing groups seek their own revolutions in a multiplicity of possible arrangements.

This suggests a possible cause of the absolute and repressive solutions found respectively by Napoleon and Stalin in the French and Russian revolutions. Both revolutions began in good part with widespread libertarian motives and reached an opposite conclusion. The intermediate struggles, including such modern refinements as purge trials, may reflect the forceful elimination of alternative solutions. The model suggests also the rationale of democratic socialist gradualism which seeks to avoid the problem of restoring order by making changes in the direction of socialism without upsetting the whole order at once. This of course is speculation quite apart from the strict mathematical treatise.

In military affairs the theory of games is more highly developed and exact. Its application in military science is one of the preoccupations of the U.S. Air Force's "Project Rand," which is now conducted by the Rand Corporation, an independent, non-profit, research organization of ranking scientists in Santa Monica, California. The theory has also been taken up by the Navy and is having its Army genesis in the "Eisenhower Advanced Study Group."

The military application of "Games" was begun early in

the past war, some time in fact before the publication of the complete theory, by ASWORG (Anti-Submarine Warfare Operations Research Group, predecessor of the Navy's present Operations Evaluation Group). Mathematicians in the group had got hold of von Neumann's 1928 paper on game theory. The success of their work led to the present Naval and Air Force applications, which are hidden behind military security. Something, however, can be said about them.

Most military problems are two-person games. They can be reduced to such game types as the duel, deployment, and the search. Problems of the last type, involving a contest between airplane and submarine, first preoccupied ASWORG when submarines were destroying our transport.

The search problem is described by Philip M. Morse, director of ASWORG, in the *Bulletin* of the American Mathematical Society (July, 1948), as follows:

"An observer, equipped with some means of making contact with a target, moves or is moved over an area of volume in some more or less regular pattern of search; the problem is to find the pattern which most efficiently results in contact under specified circumstances. The problem is applicable to many cases: the means of contact may be visual, by radar or sonar; the means of transport of the observer may be by aircraft or beneath the water; the 'observer' may be a proximity-fused guided missile, and the 'contact' desired may be the destruction of the target; peacetime applications to geological prospecting are obvious, and so on . . .

"The problem usually can be divided into a number of parts: the *contact problem*, dealing with the relationship between the physical properties of the detection equipment and the probability of contact with the target, when observer and target are in given relative positions; the *track* or *pattern problem*, dealing with the determination of the optimum pattern of search for given conditions; and the *tactical problem*, dealing with the reciprocal effects occurring when the target is also provided with detection equipment. Analyses of the tactical problem often require the techniques developed by von Neumann for his theory of games. All aspects of the search problem involve fundamental concepts and techniques of the theory of probability, expressed from a point of view enough different from that of classical probability theory as to cast new light on some of its concepts and techniques."

An airplane and a submarine, for example, play poker. The submarine passes through a channel, whose length makes occasional surfacing necessary. The plane flies back and forth over the channel in an effort to detect the submarine when it surfaces. The distances are such that the plane's trips are limited. What pattern of search should the plane follow and what plan of submergence should the submarine follow? This relation of tactic to countertactic is common to most military problems. Should the plane, for example, fly the widest part of the channel with fewer trips, or the narrower parts with more trips? If the pilot chose one or the other exclusively and were found out, he would never see a submarine. The problem, in light of the theory of games, is for the pilot to find a strategy that would survive discovery and meanwhile try to find out the plans of the submarine commander in case the latter should be less discreet. This would involve a certain amount of random choice. If both are "rational," they should be able to enforce the correct strategy on each other (as the poker player did when his opponent departed from correct bluffing tactics). The correct minimax strategy for the search is very complicated—so much so that a sample solution cannot be given verbally—yet it is regarded as a relatively simple military problem. In fact, whether practical military problems can be solved by the theory of games is itself a military secret.

In the case of the duel as a model for two airplanes in combat, the problem is whether to fire early and lose ammunition or to fire late and get hit first. The amount of the opponent's ammunition is an element of strategy about which information is imperfect. Each must choose on a strategical basis when to fire. Chance moves exist only in the question whether a hit has been made. Speculation suggests that the planes, having a limited number of shots, should, on approaching each other's range, proceed a certain distance toward each other before shooting, and then shoot at certain intervals determined by random choice. It is hardly likely that a pilot would have time to cast dice in this operation, and so it appears to follow that such an operation would have to be mechanized with a chance gadget in the mechanism. And since the solution would involve vast calculations based on the functional relationship of distance and accuracy, complicated with velocities, it is hard to see how they could be worked out except by computational machines in advance of actual combat. Perhaps, in that case, the whole operation would be mechanized and there wouldn't even be a pilot. Idealized it would be a mathematician's Fourth of July show.

War, however, even push-button war, is not likely to be idealized. War is a kind of experiment, a test that generally would not be made if the opposing forces could measure accurately one another's strength. Unless there is a great disparity in the sides, the possibility of such measuring seems like daydreaming.

Even such a matter as "linear programing"—relating a specific maximum military desire for supplies to available resources—is only in the early stages of solution (this is also a general economic problem). Take this example on which the Air Force is working with game theory: The Air Force cannot always drop all the bombs it would like; military engagements have optimum, not maximum, backgrounds. At what levels, then, must various interacting activities be operated to maximize the number of tons of bombs dropped during a particular period, in view of certain constraints such as matériel and limits on the expansibility of the training and supply establishments? This can be cast as a two-person game. A typical problem of the Air Force generally requires the "maximizing" of a certain quantity, which depends on approximately 500 factors. A solution of such a problem may require several billion multiplications, solvable only with the new, high-speed electronic calculating machines.

During the past war both sides practiced a poker bluff in the shooting of dud shells. The practice grew out of the commonplace industrial problem of quality control. The elimination of defective shells in production is expensive. Someone got the idea then of manufacturing duds and shooting them on a random basis. A military commander could not afford to have a delayed time-bomb buried under his position, and he never knew which was which. The bluff made him work at every unexploded shell that came over.

A similar problem with which continental defenses are now concerned is the fact that a continent cannot be protected on a maximum basis from assault by rockets containing atomic bombs. Such rockets must be intercepted far from their targets in a very small amount of time over vast spaces. It cannot be assumed that every rocket contains an important bomb—a large proportion of them are likely to be feints, or bluffs. To mobilize full resources to destroy every one would be likely to cost more than the damage inflicted. Hence, again, an optimum would have to be achieved: an optimum system of detection and an optimum amount of interception, making it too costly for the enemy to chance the onslaught. This is also true for the "H-bomb" which simply represents a higher pay-off for a hit. War is chance and minimax must be its modern philosophy.

The theory of games may sometime have practical applications in many social fields. And yet even as theory, it has performed a service in defining the meaning of strategy.

Bibliography on Theory of Games and Economic Behavior (Chronologically Arranged)

By courtesy of Oskar Morgenstern

Theory of Games and Economic Behavior by John von Neumann and Oskar Morgenstern, Princeton University Press, 1944, xviii & 625 pages.

"Generalization of a Theorem by von Neumann Concerning Zero Sum Two-Person Games" by Abraham Wald, *Annals of Mathematics*, Vol. 46, No. 2, April 1945, pp. 281–286.

"Statistical Decision Functions Which Minimize the Maximum Risk" by Abraham Wald, *Annals of Mathematics*, Vol. 46, No. 2, April 1945, pp. 265–280.

"A Contribution to von Neumann's Theory of Games" by I. Kaplansky, *Annals of Mathematics*, Vol. 46, No. 3, July 1945, pp. 474–479.

"The Theory of Economic Behavior" by L. Hurwicz, *American Economic Review*, Vol. 35, No. 5, December 1945, pp. 909–925.

"On Weakly Ordered Systems" by M. Richardson, *Bulletin of American Mathematical Society*, Vol. 52, 1946, pp. 113–116.

"On a Theorem of von Neumann" by L. H. Loomis, *Proceedings, National Academy*, Vol. 32, 1946, pp. 213–215.

"Neumann's and Morgenstern's New Approach to Static Economics" by J. Marschak, *Journal of Political Economy*, Vol. 54, No. 2, April 1946, pp. 97–115.

"Progresos en la Teoria Economica de la Conducta Individual" by Jorge Mendez, Universidad Nacional de Colombia, *Rivista Trimestial de Cultura Moderna*, Vol. 7, July-August-September 1946, pp. 259–276.

"A Revolution in Economic Theory?" by C. Kaysen, *The Review of Economic Studies*, Vol. XIV(1), No. 35, 1946–47, pp. 1–15.

Theory of Games and Economic Behavior by John von Neumann and Oskar Morgenstern, Second Revised Edition, Princeton University Press, 1947, xviii & 641 pages.

"Foundation of a General Theory of Sequential Decision Functions" by Abraham Wald, *Econometrica*, Vol. 15, No. 4, October 1947, pp. 279–313.

"Su una Nuova Logica Economica" by Giovanni Demaria, *Giornale Degli Economisti e Annali di Economia*, Anno VI (New Series), N. 11–12, November-December 1947, pp. 661–671.

"Demand Theory Reconsidered" by Oskar Morgenstern, *Quarterly Journal of Economics*, Vol. 62, No. 2, February 1948, pp. 165–201.

"Poker: An American Game" by John McDonald, *Fortune*, Vol. 37, No. 3, March 1948, pp. 128–131 & 181–187.

"The Theory of Games" by Richard Stone, *Economic Journal*, Vol. 58, No. 230, June 1948, pp. 185–201.

"The Utility Analysis of Choices Involving Risk" by Milton Friedman and L. J. Savage, *Journal of Political Economy*, Vol. LVI, No. 4, August 1948, pp. 279–304.

"Some Notes on the Structure of the Duopoly Problem" by Hans Brems, *Nordisk Tidsskrift for Teknisk Økonomi*, Nos. 1–4, 1948.

"Theory of Games and Economic Behaviour" by G. Leunbach, *Nordisk Tidsskrift for Teknisk Økonomi*, Nos. 1–4, 1948.

"Oligopoly, Monopolistic Competition, and the Theory of Games" by Oskar Morgenstern, *Proceedings, American Economic Review*, Vol. 38, 1948, pp. 10–18.

"Wirtschaftshandlungen und Spielstrategie" by Otto Weinberger, *Statistische Vierteljahresschrift*, Band II, Heft I, Jahrgang 1949, pp. 24–31.

"The Theory of Games" by Oskar Morgenstern, *Scientific American*, Vol. 180, No. 5, May 1949, pp. 22–25.

"Theorie des Spiels" by Oskar Morgenstern, *Die Amerikanische Rundschau*, Vol. 5, August-September 1949, pp. 76–87. (Translation of paper from *Scientific American*, Vol. 180, No. 5, May 1949, pp. 22–25.)

BIBLIOGRAPHY

"Symposium on the Theory of Games" (Madison, Wisc., September 1948) *Econometrica*, Vol. 17, No. 1, January 1949:

"Recent Developments in the Mathematical Theory of Games" by E. W. Paxson, pp. 72–73.

"A Problem in Strategy" by John W. Tukey, p. 73.

"Programming in a Linear Structure" by George B. Dantzig, pp. 73–74.

"Theorie der Glücksspiele und ökonomisches Verhalten" by Oskar Anderson, *Schweizerische Zeitschrift für Volkswirtschaft und Statistik*, 85. Jahrgang, Nr. 1, Februar 1949, pp. 46–53.

"La Theorie des Jeux-Contributions Critiques à la Theorie de la Valeur" by Georges Th. Guilbaud, *Economique Appliquée*, Vol. 2, No. 2, Avril-Juin 1949, pp. 275–319.

"Speltieri och Ekonomiska Problem" by Erik Ruist, *Economisk Tidskrift*, Arg. II, Nr. 2, Juni 1949, pp. 112–117.

"The Theory of Strategy" by John McDonald, *Fortune*, June 1949, pp. 100–110.

"Bayes and Minimax Solutions of Sequential Decision Problems" by K. J. Arrow, D. Blackwell and M. A. Girschick, *Econometrica*, Vol. 17, No. 3 & 4, July-October 1949, pp. 213–244.

"Some Two-Person Games Involving Bluffing" by Richard Bellman and David Blackwell, *Proceedings, National Academy of Sciences*, Vol. 35, No. 10, October 1949, pp. 600–605.

"Equilibrium Points in n-Person Games" by John F. Nash, Jr., *Proceedings, National Academy of Sciences*, Vol. 36, No. 1, January 1950, pp. 48–49.

"Contributions to the Theory of Games" by A. W. Tucker, *The Annals of Mathematics Studies*, No. 24, Princeton University Press, 1950, p. 200: H. F. Bohnenblust, G. W. Brown, M. Dresher, S. Karlin, J. C. C. McKinsey, L. S. Shapley, R. M. Snow, D. Gale, H. W. Kuhn, A. W. Tucker, J. von Neumann, S. Sherman and H. Weyl.

"The Bargaining Problem" by John F. Nash, Jr., *Econometrica*, Vol. 18, No. 2, April 1950.

"Die Theorie der Spiele und des wirtschaftlichen Verhaltens, Part I" by Oskar Morgenstern, Jahrbuch für Sozialwissenschaft, Vol. 1, No. 2 (in press).

"Economics and the Theory of Games" by Oskar Morgenstern, *Kyklos*, Vol. 4 (in press).

"Economic Behaviour—A New Theory" by K. George Chacko, *Indian Journal of Economics* (in press).

128